LARGE MAMMALS OF THE CENTRAL ROCKIES

LARGE MAMMALS OF THE CENTRAL ROCKIES

A GUIDE TO THEIR LOCATIONS AND ECOLOGY

Stephen C. Torbit, Ph.D.

ISBN: 0-9618450-0-7

Library of Congress Catalog Card Number: 87-70892

Bennet Creek Publications
P.O. Box 802
Monte Vista, Colorado 81144

Printed in the United States
Robinson Press, Fort Collins, Colorado, 80524.

DEDICATION

I would like to dedicate this book to the numerous people who made it possible:

To my great-grandfather
   He taught me to respect the past and all living things.

To my grandparents and parents
   They taught me that the land does not belong to man, man belongs to the land.

To Francis and Evelyn Clark
   For opening the gates to Bennet Creek to me.

To my wife, Karen
   For sharing many of my wildlife adventures.

To my daughter, Heather
   May she never know a Colorado without wild places and wild creatures.

What is man without the beasts?

*If all the beasts were gone, men
would die from a great loneliness
of spirit.*

*For what happens to the beasts soon
happens to man.*

All things are connected.

Chief Seattle

TABLE OF CONTENTS

INTRODUCTION

This book was published in response to the many questions I have received over the years from people anxious to observe wildlife. This guide will help you locate and identify large mammals inhabiting the central Rockies. Additional information is supplied to help you understand some of the ecological adaptations that allow these animals to successfully inhabit Rocky Mountain ecosystems.

My objective is not only to help you to observe wildlife, but also to help you understand what you see and thereby increase your appreciation of wild creatures and the wildlands they inhabit. Hopefully, this increased appreciation will build into an advocacy for wildlife and the habitats that they cannot live without. Your involvement in conservation issues will assure that future generations will also be able to enjoy free-ranging wildlife.

Geographical Context

The central Rockies of Colorado are the primary focus for this book. However, many of these animals can be located in similar habitats in neighboring states.

This guide is designed to help you recognize key habitats that support large mammals. Beyond that, general locations (National Forests, mountain ranges, drainages, etc.) are listed that are known to be inhabited by these mammals. A general Colorado road map and U.S. Forest Service map will provide adequate detail for you to begin to locate the desired species.

The best opportunities to observe wildlife are found in National Parks and Monuments. The most detailed locations for wildlife observation in this book are provided for lands administered by the National Park Service, specifically; Rocky Mountain National Park, Florissant Fossil Beds

Elk and Bear Sign. The scars on the lower half of the tree are from elk eating the bark. The claw marks of a black bear continue on up the trunk. Rocky Mountain National Park.

1

National Monument, and Great Sand Dunes National Monument. Key areas to observe wildlife are tied to specific landmarks shown on maps provided at the entrances to these three federal parks.

I have included a recommended reading list in the back of this book. These recommended publications will allow you to examine a specific topic in much more detail. Special references for each specie are supplied, as well as a recommended tracking guide.

Dimensions of animals, tracks and feces, and animal weights are given in metric units. These units are followed by the English equivalent. The world is converting to the metric system and, to that end, metric units are provided. Metric abbreviations are used throughout the text. These abbreviations are: kg—kilogram; mm—millimeter; cm—centimeter; km—kilometer.

How to Observe Wildlife

This book cannot guarantee that you will be successful in observing the large mammals listed. The key ingredients in determining your success are patience and persistence. You may have to wait long hours on many return visits to view the animals described in this book. However, I can assure you that the more time you spend in the environment, the more you will see and the more you will understand about wildlife and wildlife habitats.

Early mornings and late evenings are the best times to view large mammals. Most mammals are nocturnal (night active) or crepuscular (twilight active); therefore, you must be in place and ready to begin observations at these times. Observation of the hoofed animals will probably be your first successes. These animals allow themselves to be seen more easily (especially during winter). It will take both extra work and luck to observe the predators described here. Predators are solitary animals that are most active at night. Additionally, these are the animals that most severely compete with

man and his agricultural interests. Therefore, predators generally have found that their lives are extended by simply avoiding people. None of us may ever have the opportunity to observe free-ranging grizzlies or wolves in Colorado again. In my mind's eye at least, I can still see some last secret place in this state that may be remote and wild enough to be inhabited by these creatures. However, both species are described here to provide a reference point for observations of other carnivores.

Wild animals do leave behind evidence of their presence, and as you become more familiar with their "sign," you will increase your chances of observing animals. Look for claw marks on aspen trees from bears and tooth marks from elk that have stripped away aspen bark. Check out stream sides and pond shores for tracks of animals that have come to water or hunt. Be sure to look for tracks in the snow. By following tracks in the snow, not only will you be able to verify what mammals use the area, but you will also be able to read the story of hunting encounters or winter play activities. Finally, become familiar with the different kinds of fecal material or "scat" that is left behind by wildlife. Herbivores will leave groups of fecal pellets behind, while predators will deposit scat that is frequently full of hair, feathers, and bones. You will be able to identify the type of prey consumed by predators by examining their scat. Be forewarned, some surprises may result. During summer, grasshoppers and berries may be found in coyote scat and, during winter, parts of elk or even a popcicle stick may be discovered.

Special Regulations

For some of the species described in this book, special regulations are listed for the National Parks and Monuments. Please abide by these rules! These regulations have been established not only to ensure that everyone has an equal opportunity to enjoy wildlife, but also serve to provide some secure spots, free from harassment, for the creatures. It is illegal to remove any natural, archeological, or historic item from a national park. This includes dead animals and shed antlers. Please let others feel the joy of discovery. "Take only photos, leave only footprints." By abiding by these rules and regulations, you can be assured these populations will be viable for years to come. In areas where no specific regulations exist, please use common sense and courtesy when trying to observe wildlife. Never chase the animals—let them come to you. Don't whistle or throw rocks just to get an animal to raise its head. Never approach these animals too closely, they are large and dangerous and may react aggressively if you press too closely. Never feed any wildlife or use food as bait to attract them near to you. Leave your dog at home or in the car under control. Wildlife and dogs simply do not mix; it will be better for all concerned to leave your dog behind. Simply be persistent and patient, and you will be more successful than you can imagine.

Wildlife Photography

A good way of preserving your observations of wildlife, their sign and habitats, is to record what you see with a 35 mm camera. Huge telephoto lenses are not required to capture wildlife on film. I recommend lenses in the 200 mm range, and the largest I would recommend would be a 400 mm. Begin with the smaller lenses and they will force you to sharpen your skills in stalking and waiting for animals. Long lenses are no substitute for being close to animals. Since most animals are active when the light is poor, shorter focal length lenses will provide better light gathering capabilities than their large counterparts. Tripods and gun-stocks are useful for holding the camera steady under poor light conditions.

A wide variety of film is available for you to capture wildlife. Most of the photos included here were shot on Ektachrome film, the remainder on Kodachrome film. Medium speed films (ASA 64 or 100) will produce the best results, but you may need to have a few rolls of high-speed film (ASA 200 or greater) on hand to capture exciting events in poor light.

A visit to the Denver Zoo and Museum of National History will give you the opportunity to observe all of the animals discussed here and practice with your camera. The general public usually perceives these animals to be much larger than they are in reality. A visit to these two or similar institutions will allow you to see the size and color of the animals at close range and permit you to see what magnification your camera lens provides. You will begin to appreciate how difficult close-range wildlife photography is, especially when you desire consistently high quality photos. You will also be able to view mounted specimens of animals that may no longer inhabit the central Rockies. For example, a family group of Colorado grizzlies is on display at the Denver Museum of Natural History.

Your camera will test your patience, it is always better to allow the animals to approach you than to chase after them. Your vehicle makes an excellent photographic blind. Simply turn off the engine, be quiet, and allow the animals to approach. Camouflage clothing will help hide the human form when you are out hiking, and scents which mask human odor will also increase your chances of success.

PLANT COMMUNITIES

Plants form the basis for all life on earth, not only because they "fix" the sun's energy into more usable forms, but they also produce the oxygen necessary for the combustion of that energy. Ecologists generally describe wildlife habitats according to the type of plant community forming that habitat. I have briefly described below some of the more general plant communities and, therefore, wildlife habitats found in the central Rockies. These descriptions are not detailed, but are designed to provide you with keys to recognize different habitats and anticipate the large mammals that inhabit them.

Shortgrass Prairie

The shortgrass prairie is found east of the Rocky Mountains and is dominated by blue grama grass *(Bouteloua gracilis)* and buffalo grass *(Buchloe dactyloides)*. Climatic factors that help determine this community's structure are the meager precipitation (exists in the rain shadow formed by the Rockies) and constant wind. Only along stream courses and ponds are cottonwood trees *(Populus sargentii)* and willows *(Salix spp)* or other shrubs found. This habitat has been extensively disturbed by man, by livestock grazing, conversion to cropland, and urbanization.

Cold Desert Shrublands

This habitat type is found in intermountain parks, western Colorado, and the San Luis Valley. The characteristic vegetation is sagebrush *(Artemsia tridentata)*. This habitat is moister and colder than the shortgrass prairie and provides important wintering areas for many large mammals. In the San Luis

Aspen in Early Winter. Note the abundance of vegetation under the aspen and scars from elk on the trunk. Horseshoe Park, Rocky Mountain National Park.

Valley, this habitat is dominated by greasewood *(Sarcobatus vermiculates)* and rabbitbrush *(Chyrsothamnus spp)*, little sagebrush is present. Unlike sagebrush, greasewood and rabbit brush are not important forages for wildlife.

Pinon-Juniper Woodland

This woodland is dominated by piñon pine *(Pinus edulis)* and Rocky Mountain juniper *(Juniperus scopulorum)*. It is found at moderate elevations in southern and western Colorado. The understory is only sparsely covered by forbs and grasses, and yet this habitat provides important winter range. On the eastern slope, this habitat grades into the shortgrass prairie, while on the western slope it blends into the sagebrush steppe.

Mountain Shrub

This community is usually found below the montane forests and is characterized by a variety of shrubs. In the northeastern Colorado foothills, bitterbrush *(Purshia tridentata)*, mountain mahogany *(Cercocarpus montanus)*, plum *(Prunus americana)*, and chokecherry *(Prunus virginiana)* not only dominate the mountain shrub type, but provide important food for large mammals.

In the southeastern foothills, the mountain shrub type intermingles with the piñon-juniper type. The major shrub here is oakbrush *(Quercus gambelii)*, although some sagebrush occurs. On the western slope, serviceberry *(Amelanchier alnifolia)*, bitterbrush, and rabbitbrush intermingle with oakbrush.

Montane Woodland

This type is characterized by ponderosa pine *(Pinus ponderosa)* and in moist sites, Douglas fir *(Pseudotsuga menziesii)*. The ponderosa forest is an open forest which allows significant growth of grasses, forbs, and shrubs. These open woodlands are important feeding sites for some large mammals during winter.

Subalpine Forest

In Colorado, one usually associates the subalpine forest with Engelmann spruce *(Picea engelmanii)* and subalpine fir *(Abies lasiocarpa)*. Limber pines *(Pinus flexiis)* are found in gravelly soils on exposed ridges and lodgepole pine *(Pinus contorta)* may be found in dense stands where a disturbance has occurred (usually fire). The subalpine fir and Engelmann spruce are stunted and twisted at the upper limits of tree growth and form the krummholz woodland.

Montane and Subalpine Meadows

The coniferous forests of the montane and subalpine areas are irregularly interrupted by grassy openings which westerners frequently refer to as "parks." These meadows are very important for wildlife, for here grasses and forbs dominate over trees. Not only do these areas provide important forage for herbivores, but their edges are regularly patrolled by predators on the hunt. For all mammals that utilize these parks, two important resources are immediately on hand; food and hiding cover.

Aspen Woodlands

This woodland is obviously dominated by aspen *(Populus tremuloides)*, but the lush undergrowth of forbs is also an important characteristic. Aspen woodlands are usually found in moist areas that may have experienced a disturbance.

Riparian Community

This community is water dependent and, therefore, is found along streams, ponds, marshes, and lakes. This community type does not make up a significant proportion of the landscape of Colorado; yet well over 90 percent of all animal species inhabiting Colorado utilize riparian communities during some part of their life. Aspen, willow, cottonwood, alder *(Alnus rubra)*, and seed- and fruit-bearing shrubs are important plants of this community.

Alpine Tundra

This land above treeline is characterized by low-growing vegetation, where we may find grasslands, meadows, small shrubs, and rock fellfields. The soil here is thin and poor and willows grow only in the well-watered sites where soil development is best. Freezing temperatures, wind, and intense radiation are important constraints on this type, and annual production above ground is low compared to other communities. However, the alpine is important summer range for many of the species we will discuss and some individuals even winter on the alpine.

Shortgrass Prairie. Forbs in bloom, yucca and grasses are all visible in this spring photo. Yuma county.

A. Sagebrush Steppe. Sagebrush dominate the foreground. Gunnison county.

B. Piñon-Juniper Woodland. Only piñon pines are visible in this view from the Great Sand Dunes.

C. Mountain Shrub. Oakbrush dominate this spring photo; bears were nearby. Gunnison county.

D. Ponderosa Woodland. The open ponderosa stands are also characterized by grasses, forbs, and shrubs in the understory. Rocky Mountain National Park.

C.

D.

9

A.

B.

10

A. Subalpine Forest. The subalpine forest lies immediately below the alpine tundra. Note the willows in the foreground which mark a riparian zone and the alpine in the distance. Hagues Creek, Rocky Mountain National Park.

B. Montane Meadow. The large, bare grassland in the middle of the photo provides winter forage for elk. The cliffs in the lower right are used by bighorns. Riparian vegetation dominates the upper portion of the valley. Horseshoe Park, Rocky Mountain National Park.

C. Alpine Tundra. The alpine is especially attractive in spring. Look closely and you will see strands of bighorn hair in the foreground. Rock Cut, Rocky Mountain National Park.

C.

THE CARNIVORES

The large mammals discussed in this section belong to the order *Carnivora*, which means that they all eat some flesh. Unlike herbivores, these animals have simple, chemical digesting stomachs. These digestive systems are very similar to our own, and these animals depend on food supplies that humans could consume and digest. Carnivores stand either on their toes (digitgrade) or on the sole of their foot (plantigrade) as do humans. All toes possess claws, but these are retractable in only one family. All members possess large canine teeth.

Members of this order are found near the top of the food chain and, therefore, their numbers are lower than those animals lower on the food chain (herbivores). Because these animals are near the top of the food chain, and because they have digestive systems similar to our own, they compete with man for food sources. This competition has been manifested by extensive hunting and poisoning campaigns, which has further reduced populations of carnivores and has probably led to the extirpation from Colorado of two of the species discussed in this section.

Although five families of carnivores inhabit the central Rockies, in this book we will examine members of only four families.

Mustelidae

The family *Mustelidae* includes animals that have adapted to a variety of ways of life. Some are terrestrial, others aquatic, and some live most of their lives in trees. Each foot is equipped with five toes and each toe has a non-retractable claw. The feet show the variation in the lifestyle exhibited by the whole family, some are digitigrade, others semi-plantigrade, and some plantigrade. Many species exhibit induced ovulation and delayed implantation. In other words, the female will ovulate with sexual stimulation, and the

Adult Male Coyote. The coyote has returned to feed on a yearling female mule deer that he and his mate had killed. A magpie vainly defends the carcass. Horseshoe Park, Rocky Mountain National Park.

13

fertilized egg will enter a state of suspended development. Finally, at the appropriate time, the egg will implant in the wall of the uterus and complete its growth. The family is relatively old, with fossils dating back 40 million years. Native mustelids include weasels, ferrets, mink, marten, badger, skunks, otter, and wolverine. In this book, we will examine only the largest member of this family, the wolverine.

Canidae

This is the family of dog-like carnivores with long legs and pointed snouts. The gait is digitigrade and each toe possesses a non-retractable claw. All members of this family possess a scent gland at the base of the tail. Fossils from this family date from 60 million years ago. This family is represented by dogs, coyotes, wolves, and foxes. This book will discuss only coyotes and wolves.

Ursidae

This family is characterized by omnivorous animals with large bodies and short tails. The gait is plantigrade and each front foot has non-retractable claws on each of five toes. The *Ursidae* family is closely related to the family *Canidae* and appeared as recently as 29 million years ago. Native members of this family are represented by black and grizzly bears.

Felidae

The family *Felidae* includes the highly evolved predators—the cats. These carnivores depend almost exclusively on meat for their food. The front feet are digitigrade and have five toes, each equipped with a sharp, curved, retractable claw. However, the first toe is reduced and set above the others. The hind feet have four toes, each equipped with the sharp, retractable claw. The incisors are very small and the canines very large. Fossils from this family date from approximately 30 million years ago. Native representation of this family include bobcat, lynx, and mountain lion.

Wolverine *(Gulo gulo)*

The wolverine is the largest land-dwelling member of the weasel family. For practical purposes, it looks like a small bear with a large, bushy tail. The tail is frequently one-fourth the length of the body. Wolverines are a rich, dark brown color with very distinctive cream or yellow stripes along their sides. The stomach is usually a lighter brown with yellowish white spots on the throat and chest. A "mask" may be observed about the eyes. Adults average 1000-1200 mm (39-47 inches) in total length and 11-28 kg (25-60 pounds). These animals usually appear larger because of their heavy, bushy fur. Females are smaller than males, but sexes are not easily distinguished.

Breeding:

Females apparently breed as yearlings during their second summer. Implantation is delayed until January when two to four fertilized eggs implant in the uterus. The young are born in March in a sheltered den and usually leave the den by May and stay with their mother for two years. This low rate of reproduction makes wolverines vulnerable to over-exploitation and slow population recovery.

Sign:

All five toes and claws may be revealed in a perfect track in snow or soft mud. Frequently, only four toes appear in the track, which is 10-17 cm (4-7 inches) long. The heel pad may show two lobes, a large front lobe and a small circular rear lobe. Wolverines move with a loping gait. The scat of wolverines is not distinctive. It may be 12-17 cm (5-7 inches) long, semi-segmented, and full of hair and bone.

Habits and Habitat:

The wolverine is a circumpolar animal, occurring in northern latitudes in both the old and new worlds. Very little is known about wolverines since they are secretive, wide-ranging animals. Even less is known about the habits and status of wolverines in Colorado, and most of the information presented here comes from observations further north. Wolverines were probably never abundant in Colorado, which represents the southern limits of their distribution. Historical observations place the wolverine in suitable habitat from Wyoming to New Mexico. Wolverines are animals of the heavy boreal forest and tundra. In Colorado, they previously occurred throughout the mountains in the spruce-fir forests and alpine tundra. Wolverines may be territorial and have very large home ranges of 200 square km (500 square miles) which would typically include one male and two or three females.

Wolverines consume a variety of animal material (including invertebrates) and occasionally nuts and berries. Although they regularly hunt for food, carrion is apparently an important food source, especially during winter. They have the reputation of raiding trap lines and human food caches. Wolverines can hunt by a variety of methods since they are adept at climbing trees and digging for rodents. During winter, when ungulates are hampered by deep snow, wolverines are apparently capable of successfully taking large herbivores. Their use of carrion undoubtedly led to their decline in Colorado when poison baits were set for wolves, bears, and coyotes and consumed by wolverines. Wolverines are very defensive around food sources and when threatened. These animals have been reported to drive bears and lions from kills and are referred to as "devils of the north" in Canada and Alaska.

Locations

The current status of wolverines in Colorado is uncertain. In 1979, a male wolverine was killed along the Colorado-Utah border. The most likely areas that still support wolverines include the San Juan Mountains (Weminuche and South San Juan Wilderness), the southwestern portion of the Flat Tops Wilderness, the Mount Zirkel Wilderness, and along the north and west boundary of Rocky Mountain National Park. In the late 1970s this author observed a wolverine for several minutes hunting on the alpine just outside the northwest corner of Rocky Mountain National Park. Wolverines are currently designated as endangered in Colorado, therefore, it is illegal to take a wolverine. Hopefully, this protection has not come too late to maintain a viable population of this wilderness animal in the central Rockies.

Coyote *(Canis latrans)*

Coyotes resemble a very furry, medium-sized dog. The ears are erect and the nose more pointed and tail bushier than most dogs. Coyotes are generally gray or grizzled on their head, back, and sides, but the belly is usually white. The ears, legs, and feet are rusty, and the tail is black tipped. Coyotes usually hold their tails down when standing and always while running. This trait is distinctive, for wolves carry their tails straight out when running.

Coyotes stand 60-70 cm (24-28 inches) at the shoulder and are 105-140 cm (42-56 inches) in total length. Coyotes usually weigh between 10 and 20 kilograms (20-44 pounds); however, larger individuals have been documented. Female coyotes are smaller than males.

Sign:

Coyote scat is dog-like in appearance. It is cylindrical with one pointed end. The scat can be composed of a variety of materials. Some are entirely composed of vegetation (mostly grasses), others are full of grasshoppers or other insects. During winter, coyote scat is usually devoid of vegetable material and is composed of the hair and bones of its hunting victims.

Coyote tracks are longer than wide and usually form a straight line. Tracks are usually 6.5 cm (2.5 inches) long and 5 cm (2 inches) wide. Four toes with blunt claws are revealed in perfect tracks; however, claws do not always register. A coyote stride averages 33 cm (13 inches) when walking.

Breeding:

Coyotes breed in January and February, and the young are born in a den 60-65 days later. Any sheltered place may be used for a den; a hollow log, cave, or burrow. Dens are usually within sight of regular hunting trails. Coyotes may prepare several dens so that, if disturbed at one location, they can move to another. The 4-6 young are blind and helpless at birth. At three weeks of age, the pups begin to explore the den's opening. The den is abandoned when the pups are eight to ten weeks old. The family hunts as a group until fall when some of the young may leave the family.

Habits and Habitat

Coyotes successfully exploit every habitat found in the central Rockies, although they may only use some on a seasonal basis. Open meadows, grasslands, riparian areas, and forest edges are the most frequently hunted areas. These canids retreat to sheltered forests or canyons during the day to rest.

As indicated by the composition of their scat, coyotes will eat virtually anything. Rabbits, hares, mice, voles, marmots, squirrels, and birds are eaten. In other words, essentially all animals smaller than the coyote are potential prey. Larger prey (deer and elk) are occasionally taken during winter when snow and ice make them more vulnerable to predation. Carrion is probably the most important source of food during winter.

Coyotes hunt alone, in pairs, and in packs. A pair of coyotes working as a team is capable of bringing down adult deer, and a pack of five to seven coyotes may be successful in killing elk. I have observed pairs bringing down deer and packs taking elk in Rocky Mountain National Park. Groups will frequently vocalize together before they set out to hunt. This yapping and howling in the evening is a welcome sound to many wildlife observers. During winter, coyotes use areas of hard-packed snow and ice as travel routes. Therefore, one can frequently observe coyotes or their sign on frozen rivers, lakes and ponds, and along plowed roads or trails packed by the wind or skiers.

Coyotes have expanded their range throughout the continent in spite of being severely persecuted by humans. Coyotes do occasionally kill domestic livestock; therefore, they are trapped, poisoned, hunted from the air, and killed in their dens. Despite man's attempt to control coyotes, they have prospered because they are very adaptable and will eat almost anything. Therefore, if one type of prey is reduced, they simply switch to a new prey target. Another factor which has contributed to the coyote's success has been the elimination of the wolf. Wolves and coyotes are enemies and wolves are very successful in keeping coyote numbers in check.

Locations

Coyotes occur in all habitats of the central Rockies, but are probably more abundant in remote prairie and mountain areas. They can be encountered anywhere, even at the edge of cities. Coyotes are classified as furbearers and may be legally taken in Colorado.

Rocky Mountain National Park. Coyotes can be most frequently observed during winter in the open parks in Rocky Mountain National Park. Preferred locations for coyote observation are:

Horseshoe Park	—summer and winter
Endo Valley	—summer and winter
Beaver Meadows	—summer and winter
Moraine Park	—summer and winter
Sprague Lake	—winter
Upper Poudre River	—summer
Trail Ridge Road	
Between Sundance Mountain	
and Lava Cliffs	—summer
Kawuneeche Valley (upper)	—summer
(lower)	—winter

Florissant Fossil Beds National Monument. Best locations to observe coyotes at

Florissant are along the Hornbek Wildlife Loop Trail and the Hans Loop Trail.

Great Sand Dunes National Monument. Coyotes can actually be observed on the main dune field at the Great Sand Dunes. However, best opportunities are along the edges of the dune field where it meets the pinon-juniper woodland. Brushy areas immediately south of the main dune field are also good areas to watch for coyotes. Drainages east of the main dune field (Medano, Castle, and Mosca creeks) should be searched for coyotes and their sign.

Coyotes also inhabit Mesa Verde National Park, Dinosaur, Black Canyon, and Colorado National Monuments.

Gray Wolf *(Canis lupus)*

The gray wolf is the largest member of the dog family and is circumpolar in its distribution. These animals are more robust than coyotes in every dimension. Their heads are massive, legs long, and the chest deep. Adults average 45-50 kg (100-110 pounds) and females are slightly smaller than males. Wolves stand 60-100 cm (24-40 inches) at the shoulder and have a total length of 95-210 cm (38-83 inches). Their faces are more dog-like in appearance than coyotes, and the nose pad is larger. There is a great variation in the color of wolves, all shades between white and black occur. However, a grizzled-gray color predominates over most of the animal's range.

Although occasionally wolves live a solitary existence, they are social animals that have evolved cooperative hunting strategies. Packs are composed of a dominant breeding pair and their offspring. The size of the family unit expands as young are brought into the pack and contracts as juveniles disperse in search of their own territories.

Sign

Wolf tracks resemble those of a domestic dog, but are more robust. The fore-print averages 12 cm (5 inches) in length and is slightly narrower in width. The hind-print is somewhat smaller and may partially obscure the fore-print. A perfect track will show four toes with blunt claws and a lobed heel pad. In winter, hair between the toes will cause the toe prints to nearly touch each other Wolf scat is cylindrical and very similar to a domestic dog's scat. The scat will show the undigested remains of hunting victims and is used to mark the boundaries of a pack territory. Rendezvous sites are also characteristic of wolves. These resting areas are usually located where visibility is good and are recognized by numerous tracks, scat deposits, heavily used trails, beds, and food caches.

Breeding

Wolves breed in February and March and the pups arrive 60-65 days later. Dens are excavated in a bank or hill top. The pups emerge from the den at about one month of age and approach all pack members to beg for food. The pups "mouth" the muzzle and throat of returning hunters to stimulate the regurgitation reflex in the adults. The partially digested food is then consumed both by the pups and their "baby sitter"—usually the dominant female. By late summer the pups join the pack to begin their training as hunters. The young are sexually mature in two years, but breeding is delayed (especially in males) until social dominance is attained.

Habits and Habitats

Wolves once ranged extensively over North America, but now their range is generally restricted to Canada and Alaska. Wolves are opportunistic predators that will take small mammals and birds, even insects if the opportunity presents itself. However, the cooperative hunting skills of the pack lend themselves more effectively to hunting large, hoofed animals. Wolf packs prey on deer, elk, moose, sheep, caribou, muskoxen, even bison. The right circumstances must be present before an encounter leads to a hunting attempt, and large animals find themselves more vulnerable to wolf predation during winter when they are weak or immobilized by deep snow. Wolves cover great distances in search of their prey, the radius of their hunting territory may be as large as 156 km (60 miles). Wolves are usually nocturnal in their hunting forays, but may be active during daylight hours in winter.

Locations

Two types of wolves once ranged over the central Rockies. "Buffalo" wolves roamed the plains and "timber" wolves the mountains. Wolves were reported from every county in Colorado at the turn of the century, although their numbers were severely reduced over historical levels. Wolves were particularly abundant in North, Middle, and South Parks, probably because of the bison herds that also roamed these parks. Other areas known to have historically supported relatively high populations of wolves were the White River drainage, the Gunnison Basin, and the San Juan Mountains.

Two factors led to the decline of wolves throughout all the Rocky Mountain states. The destruction of the large hoofed animals by market hunters and settlers severely restricted the available prey base. As settlers brought livestock west, they also brought their fear and hatred of wolves. Wolves began to prey on livestock as their native prey populations were eliminated. Trapping and poisoning campaigns were then mounted against wolves by livestock interests (including the federal government). The result, wolves were eliminated from the west by the mid 1940s. The last confirmed wolf in Colorado was killed in Conejos county in 1943. Although reports of scattered individuals persist in the central Rockies (principally from the San Juan Mountains), there is no verified evidence that viable wolf populations exist. A former federal trapper reported a wolf in Saguache Park (Saguache County) in 1967. Wolves are currently classified as endangered in Colorado, but this protection, like that afforded to the grizzly, has been very convenient in its tardiness and has come too late. However, the National Park Service is currently evaluating the feasibility of restoring the wolf to Yellowstone National Park. If successful in Yellowstone, wolves may be considered for reintroduction in Rocky Mountain National Park. If that event occurs, then we may all have the chance to catch the wispy form of a wolf as it moves along the timber on a winter night, illuminated by a full moon, or to experience the chorus of a pack howling as they begin to ready themselves for the evening's hunt.

Black Bear *(Ursus americanus)*

Black bears are the most familiar bear to the North American public. Although their distribution is not continuous, they are found from the Atlantic to the Pacific and Alaska to Mexico. Their wide distribution has contributed to the public's familiarity with this bear.

Large black bears may attain a weight of 227 kg (500 pounds) and a length of 188 cm (6+ feet). However, most males average 120 kg (265 pounds) prior to denning and 160 cm (5 feet) in length. Females are significantly smaller, averaging 130 cm (4.25 feet) and usually weigh less than 90 kg (200 pounds). The tail is short and stubby and doesn't contribute significantly to the overall length.

Black bears can be almost any shade of color from black to white. In the central Rockies colors of individuals vary from black to chocolate, cinnamon to red. Visitors frequently confuse the cinnamon phase with the color of a grizzly. Black bears frequently have a white blaze on the chest. The snout and muzzle is always tan and the face has a straight or "Roman nosed" appearance. These characteristics help to distinguish black from grizzly bears.

Sign

Fore and hind prints of bears are quite different. The hind print resembles that of a barefoot human, while the fore print shows the toes and a short, square-shaped pad. Both fore and hind prints average 13 cm (5 inches) wide; however, the hind prints are 18 cm (7 inches) long and the fore prints 11 cm (4.5 inches) long. Claws usually do not register on black bear tracks; if they do, they are short, about the length of a toe pad. Bear feet have the large toe on the outside of the foot and small toe on the inside. The small toe may fail to register a track on a hard surface.

Black bear scat is dark, copious, and roughly cylindrical. A variety of materials may occur in black bear scat; vegetation (primarily grasses), berries, insects, hair, bone, nuts, and wood fragments. If the bear has fed heavily on berries, the scat is very liquid and virtually black. No material which was excavated and then eaten appears in black bear scat; tubers, roots, bulbs, etc., are a characteristic of grizzly bears.

Black bears climb and mark trees. Aspen trees hold the scar of a black bear claw with fine detail. Bark of coniferous trees is clawed and ripped to access the nutritious inner bark. However, overturned rocks and logs, or stumps and logs torn apart, or berry patches with broken limbs are all signs of black bear feeding sites.

Breeding

Black bears breed in late May or early June. Implantation is apparently delayed until the female enters her den (early November). The cubs (2-6) are born in January or February and are very small and helpless. The cubs average 250 grams (9 ounces) at birth, but build their weight to about 2 kg (4.5 pounds) when the den is abandoned. The young are aggressively protected by their mothers and are sent scurrying up a tree at the first hint of danger. The family spends the entire summer and fall together and even den together the following winter. The family breaks up the following spring when the female comes into heat again. Females do not usually breed until they are three or four years old, sometimes older. Delayed sexual maturation and alternate-year breeding significantly reduce the reproductive potential of black bears.

Habits and Habitats

As previously stated, black bears were once found from coast to coast, except in desert areas. Black bears are forest-dwelling animals, but in the central Rockies, trees are most important for escaping danger. The understory of our forests is the key in determining bear abundance, for the understory supplies most of their food. Black bears are more common in plant communities that produce berries, nuts, nutritious forbs, and succulent grasses. The mountain shrub community is very important for black bears in Colorado, especially oakbrush stands, for here they can find acorns to feed upon. Riparian corridors and wet meadows also provide important feeding sites, as do avalanche chutes. Chutes are important because the bears can occasionally find animals killed by the avalanche, and the avalanche continuously sets back plant succession, discouraging the coniferous forest from invading. Finally, piñon-juniper woodlands provide important piñon nuts for bears, and aspen groves provide an excellent understory where a hungry bear might find clover, strawberries, insects, or flowers upon which to feed.

As you can gather from the preceding discussion, black bears eat a variety of foods, plants, insects, fruits, fish, and mammals. Young deer, elk, or moose are actively hunted in the spring in some areas, and black bears can occasionally become important in reducing production in some herds. Carrion is also utilized, especially when the bears abandon their den. It is very advantageous for bears to find a good source of high-protein food when breaking their winter fast. Black bears will kill livestock for food and utilize livestock as carrion. These habits have brought the wrath of many a rancher on black bears; all too frequently the bear was feeding on an animal that was already dead. Black bears will utilize human food and garbage and become accustomed to humans around garbage dumps and other areas of food concentration. These habits frequently cause a conflict with humans and, again, the bear usually loses.

The end of the growing season signals the coming of hard times for bears, so they have evolved a mechanism that allows them to survive these times of food shortage. Bears "sleep" in a den during the long winter and live off of their stored fat supplies. Bears do not actually hibernate, since they can be easily aroused, and their body temperature does not drop but a few degrees below normal. Pregnant females not only must sustain themselves during denning, but also must supply adequate milk for their hungry cubs. By delaying the implantation of fertilized eggs, the female assures that the amount of nursing time in the den is minimized, thus helping to ensure that she and her cubs have the best chance of surviving the winter. Bears leave their dens in March and April in search of high-quality foods to "restart" their digestive and urinary systems. Bears neither urinate or defecate during their winter dormancy and, therefore, it requires a little time to get these systems back in working order. Dens are typically rock shelters, logs, or holes under the base of trees or shrubs.

Bears are normally solitary except for family groups, breeding pairs, and congregations around concentrated feeding sites (fishing streams, garbage dumps, etc.). Bears are probably not territorial, but do have a form of social hierarchy. At concentrated feeding sites, females with cubs are near the top of social order, allowing only the largest, most aggressive males to displace them.

Bears are probably more active during night than the day, but can be observed at any time. Since bears are shy and travel long distances between feeding sites, they are not frequently observed. When bears are encountered, one must exercise caution for these animals can be dangerous, especially a mother with cubs, when feeding on carrion or other important food sites, or when mating.

Bears are currently classified as a big game animal in Colorado and can be legally hunted during the spring and fall.

Locations

In Colorado, black bears are generally found west of Interstate 25. They are found east of I-25 in Huerfano and Las Animas counties. Western Colorado generally has more abundant black bear populations, due to higher precipitation. Areas known to support black bears in moderate numbers include Jackson, Routt, Grand, Eagle, Pitkin, Gunnison, Montrose, Hinsdale, Montezuma, La Plata, Mineral, Archuleta, and Conejos counties.

Rocky Mountain National Park. Fire suppression has reduced the value of habitats for black bears in RMNP. Rocky was always better grizzly habitat than black bear habitat, and the suppression of fires has seriously reduced the number of black bears utilizing RMNP. However, black bears do inhabit RMNP and are occasionally seen at the following locations:

North side of Sundance Mountain
Chapin Pass
Below Alpine Visitors Center
Hidden Valley
Never Summer Mountains
North slope of Long's Peak
Wild Basin
Copeland Lake

Florissant Fossil Beds National Monument. Bear sign is frequently seen in the southwest quarter of the monument, especially in the vicinity of the Hans Loop Trail.

Great Sand Dunes National Monument. Bears forage for piñon nuts along the eastern boundary of the monument. They are occasionally observed near the Mosca Pass Trail and along Medano Creek.

Grizzly Bear *(Ursus arctos)*

The grizzly is the largest carnivore native to the central Rockies and the subspecies inhabiting coastal Alaska is the largest land carnivore in the world. Unfortunately, the general public perceives all grizzlies as huge giants, capable of incredible destruction. This view is largely the result of gross exaggerations by Hollywood film makers, who sell more tickets the more terrifying the attraction. The majority of first-time observers are disappointed in the size of free-roaming grizzly bears.

Adult grizzlies stand 90-122 cm (3-4 feet) at the shoulder and measure 180-214 cm (6-7 feet) in length. Females are usually smaller than males. Adults range from 114-275 kg (250-600 pounds), although larger specimens have been recorded. The heaviest bear captured by the Craigheads during their grizzly research in Yellowstone was a prime male who weighed 509 kg (1120 pounds). Grizzlies may be almost any color from black to blonde; however, a light brown is probably the most common color. The long guard hairs are tipped with silver, gray, or white, and these guard hairs give the bears their "silver-tipped" or grizzled appearance. Grizzlies were not named by frontiersmen because of their overly aggressive nature or gory attacks, but because of these frosted guard hairs. Young bears frequently possess a white collar over the front shoulders and chest.

Grizzlies have several characteristics which help to distinguish them from black bears. However, none of these traits are singly diagnostic of grizzlies. A careful, patient observation lasting several minutes is necessary to identify a grizzly and photographs will help confirm an observation. Grizzlies have a hump over their front shoulders and a facial profile that is at least partially concave, the head is massive and ears rounded. Grizzlies are digging bears and their forefeet are equipped with long, curved claws. These claws can be as long as 10 cm (4 inches), but are frequently worn down to 7-7.5 cm (3.5 inches). Claws can occasionally be seen if the bear stands upright.

Sign

Grizzly bear scat is copious, usually cylindrical about 1 cm (2 inches) in diameter. The scat can contain almost any material from vegetable, animal, or human garbage sources. The presence of roots and tubers in the scat indicates an excavated feeding site and, therefore, a grizzly.

Grizzly tracks are generally the same shape as those of black bears, but more robust and larger. Tracks of black bears infrequently reveal the presence of claws, and grizzly tracks *almost* always show the marks from the claws. Generally, any bear tracks wider that 13 cm (5 inches) are grizzly tracks. However, some female grizzlies leave tracks narrower that 13 cm. Fore prints average 14 x 13 cm (5.5 x 5 inches), while hind prints average 25 x 18 cm (10 x 7 inches). It is not always possible to correctly distinguish black and grizzly tracks; therefore, caution must be exercised when encountering bear tracks.

Since grizzlies are digging bears, their excavations are diagnostic and can occasionally be located in grizzly country. These bears will excavate an enormous amount of material in search of rodents, particularly marmots. A large pit, where large boulders have been moved out, is characteristic of a grizzly at work. Grizzlies also dig day beds in thickets. These oval beds are about 90 x 122 cm (3 x 4 feet) and can be as much as 30 cm (1 foot) deep.

Grizzlies will cache large animals that they have killed or have found as carrion. These carcasses are covered with sticks, leaves, dirt, snow, or grass. If you discover a cached carcass surrounded by bear sign, back off. Grizzlies will feed off such a carcass for two to three weeks, are never far away, and will defend it with all their ferocity.

Breeding

Grizzlies mate during the same period as black bears, from May to July, with a peak in mid-June. Grizzlies are promiscuous, and a male will stay with a female only as long as she is receptive. If two males encounter a single receptive female, a vicious fight will ensue. After breeding, the fertilized eggs undergo embryonic delay and do not implant into the wall of the uterus for five to six months. The cubs (usually two) are born in their mother's den in January or February and are helpless. Birth weights of grizzlies are usually less than 0.5 kg (1 pound). However, by the time the mother abandons her den in April or May, the cubs may weigh up to 4.5 kg (10 pounds). Cubs learn what foods to eat and what enemies to avoid by spending their first summer and winter with their mother. Cubs usually disperse after spending their second winter denned with their mother. However, some cubs will actually spend a third winter denned with their mother before dispersing.

Female grizzlies frequently experience their first heat cycle when they are 3.5 years old, but are not successful breeders until they are a minimum of 5.5 years old. Some female grizzlies do not successfully breed until they are eight or nine. Females are usually productive into old age (20+ years), bearing young until they die. It is obvious that grizzlies have a very low reproductive rate and, therefore, their populations are extremely vulnerable to over-exploitation. A grizzly sow that first breeds as a five-year-old and lives to be 15 could be expected to produce a maximum of 10 cubs. Breeding females are the most important segment of the grizzly population and must be protected to maintain viable populations.

Habits and Habitats

While the black bear is a creature of the forest, the grizzly has evolved to exploit open areas. The fore claws of each specie not only provide clues to their respective lifestyles, but also how they react to threats. The short, sharp claws of black bears allow them to strip bark from trees and eat the inner bark, but they are not adequate to excavate roots and small mammals like a grizzly. When danger threatens, a black bear's claws can dig into a tree trunk and support its moderate weight as it climbs up the tree away from danger. When a grizzly is threatened, its claws will not support its great weight in a tree, and the forest is usually at some distance. Therefore, the grizzly is forced to stand its ground and confront the threat head-on. This tactic was

formerly effective against almost all threats since the grizzly is capable of killing any land dwelling animal in North America. Grizzlies were virtually immune from confrontations with native Americans. Only when confronting a bear with a group of several warriors were these primitive people capable of killing a grizzly. Even the early frontiersmen were at risk when facing a grizzly with a single-shot rifle. Only after the advent of the repeating rifle and deadly poisons did man begin to overwhelm the grizzly.

Native Americans treated the grizzly with admiration and respect. Both man and bear utilized the same food and, therefore, competed with each other for resources. Additionally, one-on-one encounters usually ended with the man losing the battle, if not his life. Grizzlies were considered powerful spirits after these early people recognized the similarity between the human form and a skinned bear. For these reasons and more, contact with grizzlies were routinely avoided unless a group of young men set out against a grizzly as a show of courage.

Despite their large size and aggressive behavior, grizzlies do not rely on meat to fill their food requirements. Rocky Mountain grizzlies depend on vegetation for the vast majority of their food. Plant material preferred by grizzlies includes grasses, clover, glacier lilies, spring beauty, strawberries, raspberries, chokecherries, serviceberries, snow berries, acorns, and pine nuts. Bears occasionally raid pine squirrel caches to acquire nuts. Grizzlies will also eat insects and virtually any animal protein—including another grizzly. Grizzlies will take young and old ungulates and regularly search for winter-killed ungulates when emerging from their winter dens. Grizzlies will expend a large amount of time hunting small mammals. Marmots comprise a meal worth active pursuit, but meadow voles, pocket gophers, ground and tree squirrels are also actively hunted. Grizzlies will take livestock if the opportunity arises and utilize a livestock carcass as it would any other form of carrion. That practice led to extensive poisoning campaigns against bears.

Undoubtedly, bears were blamed for killing much more livestock than they ever did. More frequently they were guilty of utilizing the rotting carcass.

Grizzlies were and still are feared as man-eaters. However, early naturalists (e.g. John Muir and Enos Mills) spent many years camping and traveling alone and unarmed in grizzly country. Grizzlies will try to avoid people, if at all possible. Finally, grizzlies in some areas depend on a concentrated food source (fish) which is utilized to the exclusion of all others. Bears will fish streams during the spawn and permit close association with other bears, so important is this food supply. It has been hypothesized that the enormous coastal brown bears of Alaska are simply grizzlies that have expressed the full potential of their stature because of a large, dependable supply of salmon.

Grizzlies are bears of open country, but that does not mean that they avoid timbered or brushy areas. These bears use timber as day rest areas and some foraging. However, grizzlies do spend time in the open and can be observed actively foraging there. Preferred habitats include riparian zones, sagebrush steppe, avalanche chutes, alpine meadows and rock slides, montane meadows, krummholtz and forest edges. Riparian zones are used for both travel corridors and feeding areas. Grizzlies are apparently not territorial. Home ranges of individual bears overlap each other, but bears usually encounter one another only at concentrated food sources or during the breeding season. Home ranges of grizzlies have been reported to be as small as 93 square kilometers (36 square miles) or as large as 780 square kilometers (300 square miles).

Grizzlies enter their winter dens usually in early November. Grizzlies usually dig a den under a tree on a north-facing slope. They may take advantage of a natural cavity, but will modify it to better suit their needs. Grizzlies line their dens with conifer boughs, moss, or leaves. Like black bears, grizzlies are not true hibernators, but enter a state of lethargy and sleep away the winter. They can be aroused during their winter's sleep.

Locations

Before the coming of the white man, grizzlies ranged from the Mississippi River and central Texas west to the Pacific and from Hudson's Bay and Alaska south to central Mexico. Now, however, they are essentially restricted to Canada and Alaska. Two population centers exist south of the Canadian border, Yellowstone National Park and an area of northwestern Montana, northern Idaho, and northeastern Washington. For many years a small remnant population of grizzlies was believed to exist in the San Juan mountains of southwestern Colorado.

In Colorado, grizzlies have been historically reported from every region of the state. The Journal of Jacob Fowler reports the first mortality of a white man by a grizzly in Colorado. Fowler reports the death of Lewis Dawson by a grizzly at the mouth of the Purgatoire River near the present site of Las Animas, Bent County. The presence of grizzlies along the Purgatoire was later confirmed by Major Stephen Long's expedition. Enos Mills reported extensively on grizzlies in the northern portion of the state. Grizzlies were formerly reported from all of the mountainous portion of Colorado, but seem to have been more common around North, Middle, and South Parks and the San Juans.

The Colorado Territorial Legislature actually closed the season on grizzlies in 1867, but re-opened it two years later. After the turn of the century, the exploits of several "outlaw" Colorado grizzlies routinely made the headlines. "Old Four Toes," "Old Club Foot," "Ole Mose," and others seem to have captivated the public's attention even more than the human outlaws of that time. The hide of "Old Club Foot" was a popular display at the 1904 St. Louis World's Fair. In 1915, an intensive state and federal program was initiated to eliminate grizzlies from the state. In 1922, Enos Mills published a story about a three-legged female grizzly with cubs that roamed from Berthoud Pass to Grand Lake. The "Echo Mountain Grizzly" was last observed by Mills in 1920 and was the last grizzly reported from the northern part of the state. In 1951, a two-year-old male grizzly was killed west of Creede by a federal trapper. This was considered the last confirmed grizzly taken in Colorado. For many years, numerous observations of grizzlies were reported from the head waters of the Rio Grande River and the South San Juans, but no confirmed observations could be listed. Finally, in 1973, the Endangered Species Act established absolute protection for grizzlies in Colorado and elsewhere.

For the Colorado grizzly, protection had come too late. A mere 130 years had passed from Jacob Fowler's encounter along the Purgatoire to the death of the young male west of Creede, and that was all the time it took to extirpate the grizzly from Colorado. Then, an apparition from the past appeared. Shortly after 5:00 p.m. on September 23, 1979, a bow hunter killed a grizzly in the South San Juan Wilderness at the head of the Navajo River. The bear badly mauled and nearly killed the bow hunter. This grizzly was a female estimated to have been 16 years old at the time of her death and weighed approximately 380 pounds. Retrieval of the carcass was difficult and biologists were unable to determine if she had ever had cubs. The hide and skull of this bear are currently on display at the Denver Museum of Natural History. During the two years following the death of the grizzly, the Colorado Division of Wildlife surveyed the area to determine if any other grizzlies inhabited the region. The search was inconclusive. Researchers found some old sign, but no definitive evidence of a viable grizzly population.

Did Colorado's last grizzly stand its ground against the final human intruder just as its ancestor had with the early white interlopers along the banks of the Purgatoire in 1821? As I complete this book, I am living in the shadows of the South San Juans, the last refuge of Colorado's grizzlies. I gaze upon those mountains and wonder, are there any left; is there enough room left even in these mountains for the grizzly? The pessimistic view is, unfortunately, the realistic view. It is doubtful that enough bears

exist to maintain even a small relict population. The areas set aside free from development are probably too small to support grizzlies. Meanwhile, we rush headlong into the future, a future dictated by powerful business interests that attempt to squeeze every dollar out of every acre of land. Little regard is given to the value of wildlife as a source for man's imagination or restoration of his spirit. If all the grizzlies are gone, I believe that we're all much poorer, so poor that the debt can never be erased. If all the grizzlies are gone from Colorado and the South San Juans, the mountains are only mountains, their most distinctive wilderness element has been eradicated, they are a wilderness in name only.

In 1982 the Colorado Wildlife Commission unanimously went on record opposing the reintroduction of the grizzly bear in Colorado.

Rocky Mountain National Park. Anyone interested in grizzlies in this region should read the numerous books of Enos Mills. Mills' tales take place on mountains and streams recognizable even to the casual visitor. These books make the peaks and valleys of RMNP come alive, one can almost see the ghostly forms of grizzlies lumbering along the Continental Divide.

Florissant Fossil Beds National Monument. Grizzlies undoubtedly occupied the region around FFB in historic times. In April, 1904, "Ole Mose," a famous outlaw grizzly, was killed on Black Mountain approximately 25 miles southwest of FFB. Ole Mose was reported to have killed five men and hundreds of cattle during his rein. Ole Mose was an old bear when he was killed, yet he appeared fit enough to have lived for several more years.

Great Sand Dunes National Monument. Grizzlies were known to inhabit the Sangre de Cristo Mountains in both Colorado and New Mexico in historic times. Looking southwest across the San Luis Valley, a visitor can see the South San Juans, the scene of the last stand of the Colorado grizzly.

Bobcat *(Lynx rufus)*

Bobcats are the smallest cat native to the central Rockies. Adults average 105 cm (41 inches) in total length, of which about 15 cm (6 inches) is contributed by the tail. It is this short or "bobbed" tail which has provided the common name for the cat. Adults weigh from 6-20 kg (13-44 pounds), and exceptionally large males have been reported to weigh 30 kg (65 pounds). Female bobcats are slightly smaller than the males. Bobcats of the central Rockies show considerable variation in color from red to tawny or grey. Several geographic races of bobcats converge in the central Rockies, and this results in the variety of pelage colors. Along the southern and southwestern borders of Colorado the red phase seems to predominate, while the tawny phase seems to be more typical of bobcats from the foothill and prairie areas. Grey pelage is more typical of bobcats inhabiting the higher mountain regions. It is this grey form that is confused with lynx by visitors more familiar with the reddish form common throughout the rest of the country. Regardless of the color variation, bobcats are characterized by light grey or white stomachs with distinct black spots which tend to fade along the sides and back. The back of the ear is black and the tops are tipped with short, black tufts of hair. These ear tufts are not the length of those of lynx and hence are a key to distinguish the two cats. The tail is also diagnostic since its top surface features a series of dark bands, the most distinct being the band on the top. However, these bands do not encircle the tail and the bottom of the tail is white. Lynx are identified by their single black band which encircles the tip of the tail.

Sign

Scat is infrequently observed since it is usually covered by the cats. However, cats defecate routinely at the edges of their territories and may not entirely cover feces at these scent posts. The scat is cylindrical, resembling that of a coyote; however, bobcat feces are segmented. In dry areas, the scat may separate at the segments.

Bobcat tracks are round or slightly wider than long. The diameter of these tracks averages 5 cm (2 inches), and although they generally resemble coyote tracks, bobcat tracks can be distinguished by their characteristic heel pad. The front of all cat heel pads is concave, while that of canids is convex. Prints from the hind feet are usually directly on top of fore prints. The stride of bobcats averages 28 cm (11 inches).

Breeding

The peak of the bobcat breeding season occurs in March and April. The helpless, blind young (4-6) are born about 60 days later in a sheltered rock crevice or hollow log. The female is very sensitive and may abandon the den if disturbed. The kittens' eyes open at about 10 days, and they are weaned at two months. The kittens must learn to hunt from their mother and stay with her until fall.

Habits and Habitats

Bobcats are animals of brushy, rocky, and rough terrain. They occur in all plant communities below the subalpine forest in the central Rockies. They are most common in areas of thick, brushy cover, scrub timber, and rim rock. Habitats that provide adequate food for small mammals (particularly rabbits) and hunting cover are preferred. Therefore, the best habitats to search for bobcats are the lower montane forest, piñon-juniper woodland, cold desert shrublands, riparian areas, and prairies. Thick stands of continuous forests are avoided, and large, open areas are traveled only to reach better habitats.

Bobcats are territorial. A male's territory may be as large as 52 square kilometers (20 square miles) and overlap with home ranges of females and other males. Hunting territories of females are smaller, about 26 square kilometers (10 square miles) and do not overlap territories of other females.

Bobcats will prey on any animal smaller than themselves and some that are considerably larger. They take small mammals, birds, beaver, and porcupine, but their principal prey are rabbits and hares. Large cats are capable of killing adult deer and pronghorn and will actively search for deer and pronghorn fawns and elk calves within a few weeks of the ungulate's birth. Excess food is cached, covered with sticks, leaves, conifer needles, snow, or dirt. Carrion is utilized during times of food shortage.

Bobcats fiercely defend themselves when threatened and discourage all but the most determined enemy. Mountain lions, large male bobcats, and packs of coyotes occasionally kill young bobcats. Historically, bobcats held little interest for humans, usually only when a lamb or chicken was taken. However, after western countries banned imports of fur from spotted African cats, bobcat fur became an accepted substitute. Trappers can expect as much as $350 per bobcat pelt currently. Therefore, in some parts of their range, bobcats are being overexploited for their fur. More information needs to be collected on bobcat habitat requirements to better manage their populations. Bobcats are classified as furbearers and may be legally trapped and hunted in Colorado.

Because bobcats are solitary, nocturnal, and occupy relatively large territories characterized by dense cover, they are infrequently seen. Most people, therefore, incorrectly assume that bobcats are absent. One can verify bobcats by looking for their tracks in mud or snow.

Locations

The highest bobcat densities occur in the piñon-juniper woodlands of southern and western Colorado. Oakbrush, sagebrush, and the mountain shrubland of the eastern foothills support moderate densities. Bobcats inhabit suitable habitats in all three federal parks discussed here.

Rocky Mountain National Park:

Devil's Gulch (North Fork Big Thompson)
Lumpy Ridge—Gem Lake

Fall River riparian zone
South-facing slopes above Horseshoe Park
Deer Ridge and Deer Mountain
Upper Beaver Meadows
Moraine Park riparian zone
Hollowell Park

Florissant Fossil Beds:

Hornbek Wildlife Loop (east and west trails)
Hans Loop
Cave Trail

Great Sand Dunes

Along all riparian areas
Piñon-juniper woodlands along eastern
  boundary
Medano Primitive Road (especially Point
  of No Return Turnaround)

Bobcats also range throughout Mesa Verde National Park, Dinosaur, Black Canyon, and Colorado National Monuments.

Canada Lynx *(Felis lynx)*

Canadian lynx are sometimes confused with their smaller and more abundant cousin, the bobcat. Lynx tend to be a pale gray and are frequently referred to as "pallid" in color. Lynx weigh between 5 and 18 kg (11-40 pounds) and are 70-110 cm (28-44 inches) long. Their short tail has a solid black tip, not a broken black ring as do bobcats. Long black ear tufts with ill-defined points set atop the ears. Large patches of fur that hang from the cheeks (called ruffs) are whitish with black bars. Lynx appear to be bulkier than bobcats and, although they are larger, part of their bulky appearance is due to their heavy, dense fur. The feet of lynx are large and well furred.

Sign

Lynx scat is cylindrical, tapered, and segmented, containing bones and fur. Lynx tracks are very similar in size to those of a mountain lion, but with a shorter stride (35-40 cm or 14-16 inches). The tracks are round, revealing four toes with no claws. Because fur extends onto the toes, the tracks are much larger than bobcat tracks, averaging 7.5-10 cm (3-4 inches), and frequently the toes and heel pad are obscured by the thick fur.

Breeding

Lynx breed in late winter and 2-4 kittens are born 60 days later. Kittens are probably produced every year, but many do not survive unless a plentiful prey base is available. Lynx den in any suitable sheltered place, but most frequently caves are utilized.

Habits and Habitats

Like the wolverine, lynx are wilderness animals inhabiting heavy boreal forests of the northern hemisphere and, again, Colorado represents the southern distribution of this animal. In the central Rockies, lynx are found in the upper spruce-fir and subalpine forests above 2730 meters (9000 feet), especially on north-facing slopes.

Lynx restrict themselves to spruce-fir forests because their principal prey is found there. Snowshoe hare form the primary food base for lynx although mice, grouse, and ptarmigan are also taken. Deer and elk are occasionally taken by lynx, and surplus food is covered with snow or plant litter and cached. In times of food scarcity, lynx will utilize carrion. Lynx are effective hunters of snowshoe hares during winter since lynx, also, have large feet which function as snowshoes and allow them to travel on top of deep snow without floundering. The tufts of fur on the ears act to amplify sounds of prey animals. This is important, since lynx usually hunt at night, and their hearing is a valuable hunting tool. Lynx are so tightly coupled to snowshoe hare populations that a decline in the hare population results in a similar decline in lynx numbers. Lynx populations follow the cycle of snowshoe hares and peak every nine to ten years.

Home ranges vary in size by season and prey availability. During summer and at times of large prey populations, home ranges may be as small as 10-26 square km (4-10 square miles). In winter and other times of small prey numbers, home ranges may expand to 52 square km (20 square miles).

Locations

Because of their solitary, nocturnal habits and the remote habitat they inhabit, very little is known about lynx. Historically, lynx were reported from every forest in the central Rockies, but were never common. Small lynx populations still exist in Colorado and have been recently confirmed in parts of Clear Creek, Eagle, Grand, Lake, Pitkin, and Summit counties. Lynx may be present in areas north and south of this central core. No lynx have been confirmed in any of the federal parks discussed in this book. However, I observed what may have been a pair of lynx above Milner Pass in Rocky Mountain National Park in 1983 and a lone individual on Cameron Pass (Larimer county) in 1976. Although highly prized for its long, silky fur, the lynx is classified as endangered in Colorado and may not be legally taken.

Mountain Lion (Felis concolor)

Mountain lions are the largest cat native to the central Rockies. Female lions frequently attain a total length of 2 meters (6.5 feet) and weight of 65 kg (140 pounds). Males are slightly larger, attaining a total length of 2.5 meters (8.5 feet) and weight of 95 kg (210 pounds), although males in excess of 125 kg (270 pounds) have been documented. The long, cylindrical tail of this cat is diagnostic, for it is the only native, long-tailed cat. The tail is usually 81 cm (32 inches) long and comprises about one-third of the total body length.

The color along the sides and back varies with individuals from a tawny brown to dark red. The belly and inside of the legs is a buffy-white. The face is a light brown with a black moustache and black on the backs of the ears. Although young lions are spotted, they lose their spots at 10-12 months of age.

Sign

Mountain lion tracks are round or slightly wider than long. The average front track is 9 x 10 cm (3.5 x 3.9 inches). A perfect track will show the general cat characteristic of a concave front to the heel pad. The rear of lion heel pads show three distinct lobes. When walking in snow, rear feet are planted near or precisely on front tracks. The stride of a mountain lion averages 100 cm (40 inches), and this helps distinguish lion tracks from lynx tracks. Although the size of the tracks of the two animals is similar, the stride of the lion is nearly three times that of the lynx. In deep snow, a tail drag mark will show, as will the drag marks from the paunch.

Lion scat is cylindrical, occasionally segmented, and copious, frequently as much as 0.5 liters (1 pint) of fecal material is evacuated. Hair and bones, as well as porcupine quills, may be found in the scat. Since scat is used as a territorial marker, it is frequently placed in conspicuous places and only partially covered. Male lions also leave "scrapes" where they will claw together a mound of soil or leaves and they urinate on the mound. These scrapes also function as boundary markers.

Breeding

Lions are promiscuous and may breed at any time of the year. However, there appears to be a birth peak in July, indicating that most of the breeding occurs in April. One to six cubs are born in a cave, hollow log, brush pile, or under a ledge. The cubs open their eyes after 10 days and are weaned at three months. The cubs travel with their mother and learn hunting skills until they are about two years old. At this time, they are sexually mature and must strike out on their own. Since most females breed as two-year-olds and breed only every other year, four litters

are likely the maximum production potential of a given female. The females are very protective of their young; adult male lions are known to kill and feed on cubs. If a female loses her kittens, she will come into heat within two weeks and breed again.

Habits and Habitats

The mountain lion is known by many names: cougar, puma, catamount, panther, and painter. This variety of names is due to the animal's once extensive distribution. At one time, the mountain lion was the most widely distributed mammal in the western hemisphere, ranging from the Peace River in northern Canada to Tierra del Fuego at the tip of South America and from coast to coast. As the New World was settled, lions fled into the most remote regions available, and currently the northern population is only found in viable numbers in the western U.S. and Canada.

One can easily surmise from their historic distribution that mountain lions have adapted to a variety of habitats. In the central Rockies, lions are found in areas of rugged, brushy terrain. Two of the most important habitat factors are prey availability and stalking cover. Therefore, lions are most abundant in the piñon-juniper woodlands, mountain shrub, lower montaine forest, and "badland" type habitats on the shortgrass prairie. The most predictable feature of lion habitat in the west is the presence of mule deer.

Mountain lions hunt and kill a variety of animals, small mammals and birds as opportunity permits. However, these predators have evolved the physical stature and hunting skills necessary to successfully prey on deer, bighorn sheep, and elk. Lions hunt during both daylight and night-time hours, but appear to be more active at night. Lions are not capable of running their prey down over long distances. Rather, they rely on their stealth to sneak to within 15 meters (50 feet) and then rush their prey at the precise moment. Lions depend on a last leap to propel them to a powerful collision with their prey.

Lions are tremendously strong in their front shoulders. They can absorb the shock of a collision and still cling to the prey. A broken neck or suffocation is the usual cause of death of larger prey. After the kill, the lion will remove the prey to a secluded spot to feed. If the prey is not totally consumed, the lion will cover the remains with sticks, leaves, or soil, and cache the remains. Lions will eat berries and other vegetable material, including grass, which may be consumed to promote general digestive health and reduce the load of internal parasites. Lions are primarily carnivores and must kill an average of one deer-sized animal per week to survive. Lions do kill domestic livestock, cattle, sheep, and horses. They will also kill and eat domestic cats and dogs. There are authenticated accounts of lions killing many sheep in a single night, many more than they could consume. However, western lions seem to be particularly fond of and adept at taking horses. In fact, the subspecies name for the lion inhabiting the central Rockies *(hippolestes)* means horse thief.

Lions are territorial in time and space. Several lions cannot afford to prey upon the same food resources simultaneously. Therefore, as mentioned above, lions use their scat and urine as boundary markers. These markers not only serve notice that a particular lion is in the territory, but how long since he passed by. Territories vary in size and may be as small as 26 square km (10 square miles) or as large as 260 square km (100 square miles). Lions are secretive, solitary animals that are only found together as females with young, dispersing siblings, during mating, and when two males vie for the courtship rights to a female. Fights between lions are infrequent since these solitary hunters need all of their strength and vitality for securing prey.

Lions have few enemies except when young, or when pursued by man. They can defend themselves valiantly or flee to locations inaccessible to most enemies. However, man has learned that lions will "tree" to escape barking dogs, effective to escape the dogs, but ineffective against the man at the base of the tree with a weapon. Occasional-

ly, a lion is injured or killed during an attack on a deer or elk. In spring 1985, a female lion was found dead beneath a mature bull elk she had killed near the Aspen Glen Campground in Rocky Mountain National Park. The lion had evidently been trapped underneath the bull when it died and either suffocated or died from wounds received when the elk fell and crushed her.

Although once persecuted throughout the west, lions are now considered big game and their harvest is strictly regulated. The lion bounty was abolished in Colorado in 1965.

Locations

Because individual lions avoid each other, are very secretive, avoid man, and occupy large territories, they are very difficult to observe in the wild. A pack of hunting dogs is the best way to find lions, but does not ensure success. Lions generally range west of Interstate 25 in Colorado, although recent reports from northern Weld County and along the Purgatory River hold some merit. The entire front range was formerly excellent lion habitat and lions still roam the outskirts of some front range cities. Some of the best lion habitat lies south of Cripple Creek to Canon City and Trinidad. Lions are found in fair numbers in the San Luis Valley and the San Juan Mountains. Excellent habitat is found along the southwestern border near Cortez and the Dolores River. Other excellent areas are near Grand Junction, Rifle, Meeker, Craig, and Rangely.

Rocky Mountain National Park. Lions range the lower elevations on both sides of the continental divide and have even been observed on Specimen Mountain. Best locations are: Lumpy Ridge, Deer Mountain, Deer Ridge, and the east end of Moraine Park. The canyons along the east flank of the park are known to be inhabited by lions, specifically, Devils Gulch, Big Thompson, and St. Vrain Canyons.

Florissant Fossil Beds National Monument. While lions range over the entire monument, lions are probably present most frequently off the Hans Loop Trail in the southwestern portion of the monument.

Great Sand Dunes National Monument. Lions frequent the piñon-juniper woodland on the east flank of the monument. They occasionally move to the edge of the dune fields in search of wintering mule deer.

Lions also inhabit Mesa Verde National Park, Dinosaur, Black Canyon, and Colorado National Monuments.

A. Adult Coyote. A coyote exhibiting a prime winter pelt. Horseshoe Park, Rocky Mountain National Park.

B. Adult Gray Wolf. This young male had not yet attained social dominance.

A.

B.

A.

B.

A. *Adult Black Bear. Note the brown snout and lack of shoulder hump. Larimer county.*

B. *Subadult Male Grizzly. A beautiful silvertip; note the concave facial profile and distinct shoulder hump. Yellowstone National Park.*

C. *Wolverine. Wolverines inhabit dark boreal forests and are difficult to photograph. Note the blonde, lateral stripe.*

C.

A.

B.

A. *Adult Lynx. A prime winter coat adorns this cat. Note the general gray color, dark tail band, and long ear tufts.*

B. *Adult Bobcat. This cat was caught napping. Note the reddish color and short ear tufts. Larimer county.*

C. *Mountain Lion. This cat was attracted to a predator call. Larimer county.*

C.

LARGE HERBIVORES

This section of the large mammal guide will concentrate on the large herbivores. The species described in the following section share some common characteristics which we will briefly discuss.

The large herbivores are frequently described as "ungulates," a term which refers to the fact that they walk on their unguls (hooves). Scientifically, they are classified in the order *Artiodactyla*, which means "even-toed." Therefore, we will discuss herbivores which are even-toed and walk on hooves. A keen observer will note that only four digits appear on the foot of the animals. The first digit has disappeared entirely; the animals walk on their third and fourth digits and the second and fifth digits (dew claws) have been reduced or disappeared entirely.

All wild ungulates inhabiting the central Rockies belong to the suborder *Ruminantia*. Ruminants are animals that possess complex stomachs and process their food in a complicated way. The ruminant stomach consists of four compartments; the rumen, reticulum, omasum, and abomasum. In the rumen, which is the largest compartment, the ungulate cultures microorganisms. These cultures are necessary because mammals are incapable of digesting cellulose—the structural carbohydrate found in plants. Therefore, the only way large mammals can exploit plants as food is to culture micro-organisms that are able to digest cellulose. Although this symbiotic relationship (beneficial to both organisms) is very successful, it also places serious constraints on the acquisition of energy and protein by the ungulates.

In order to efficiently culture the microbes, the culture medium (plant material) must be as small as possible. Therefore, the herbivores regurgitate their food and rechew it. This process, which is commonly known as "cud chewing," is technically referred to as rumination. After the

Bull Elk and Harem. This bull has collected several cows into his harem on the alpine. Sundance Mountain, Rocky Mountain National Park.

plant material is reduced in size, the herbivore must lie down and wait for the microbes to digest the plant material and send it along the digestive system. The abomasum is the chemically-digesting stomach of the ruminant where soluble sugars, plant proteins, and microbes are digested and start to be assimilated. This whole process takes a very long time and, if forage resources are poor (as they are during winter), it may take so long that the animal may begin to starve. However, his stomach may be almost full and he will be able to eat only a little more food. Therefore, the herbivore can starve on a nearly full stomach. Although all of the herbivores discussed in this book are ruminants, each specie is able to exploit food sources differently. Therefore, these animals have minimized competition for food resources and may be found in adjacent areas.

Ruminant forages are classed in three general categories: grasses, forbs, and browse. Grasses are easily digestible, but contain soluble sugars and proteins only during the summer. Forbs are non-woody, broad-leafed plants. Forbs are highly nutritious and easily digestible. Browse is food eaten from shrubs and trees; it contains good levels of protein, but is very difficult to digest.

Ruminants native to the central Rockies are represented by three families; cervids, bovids, and antilocaprids. These families also share some common behavioral patterns. Females, yearlings, and young usually spend winters and summers apart from mature males. This reduces forage competition between sexes of the same specie on summer and winter ranges and also reduces social stress. The males of all three families are able to determine when a female is in heat by testing her urine. The males sniff the freshly excreted urine, raise their heads, point their chins up, and curl their upper lips back. This action exposes a gland in the nasal cavity to volatile hormones. When the female is in heat, the breeding hormones alert the male that she is receptive.

Cervidae

In Colorado, cervids are characterized by those ruminants which possess no upper incisors and males that grow deciduous antlers. All males grow antlers during the spring and summer. These antlers are covered with a layer of fine hair called velvet, which protects the rich blood supply to these rapidly growing organs. The antlers harden before the breeding season and are used in displays of dominance. During mid to late winter, the antlers are shed and the cycle begins again. The family is relatively old, with fossils dating from 40 million years ago. This family is represented by mule deer, elk, moose, and, in northern latitudes, caribou.

Bovidae

This is the family to which domestic sheep, goats, and cattle belong. These herbivores are characterized by true horns in both sexes which are never shed. This family dates from fossils approximately 30 million years old. Native bovids are bison, mountain goats, mountain sheep and, in the far north, musk oxen.

Antilocapridae

This family is uniquely American and is represented by only one species—pronghorn antelope. Both sexes possess horns, although the female's horns are much smaller than the male's. The outer horn sheath is shed annually, but the bony core remains. No dew claws are present; therefore, there are only two hooves on each foot. This family is known from fossils dating back to 20 million years.

Mule Deer (Odocoileus hemionus)

Mule deer are the smallest member of the deer family native to the central Rockies. This western deer is usually larger than its eastern counterpart, the white-tailed deer. Mule deer stand about 106 cm (3.5 feet) at the shoulder. Males (bucks) are usually larger than females (does), ranging from 50-200 kg (110-440 pounds). Mule deer molt twice during the year; they are reddish in the summer and grey during the winter. Mule deer have a small, white rump patch and a short, narrow, white tail with a black tip. Black-tailed deer (found along the Pacific Coast) generally resemble mule deer, except for their tails, which are completely black on the top. Mule deer were named for their large, mule-like ears, which move independently and give mule deer a very sensitive sense of hearing.

The antlers of the males are spikes or single forks until they mature. Older males have antlers that are round and branch into a "Y" rather than having a single main beam, as do elk. The record spread for mule deer antlers is in excess of 116 cm (46 inches). Bucks shed their antlers in February, and they begin to grow a new set almost immediately. The antlers grow throughout the summer and are hardened and ready for use by late September.

Sign

Mule deer produce small fecal pellets which are deposited in a cluster or "group." An individual pellet is about 1 cm (0.5 inch) in diameter and may have a small nipple-like projection on one end and a small indentation on the other.

Mule deer tracks are the most "heart-shaped" of any of the ungulates we will examine. Tracks average 8 cm (3 inches) long and 7 cm (2.75 inches) wide. In soft surfaces, the dew claws may register in a mule deer track, especially if the deer was moving downhill. Although tracks of males are larger than those of females, it is very difficult to establish sex on the basis of tracks alone. Mule deer utilize a unique gait when they are startled and flee from danger. These deer move with a bounding, spring-like motion in which all four feet strike the ground simultaneously. This bounding motion is called stotting and allows the deer to change directions instantaneously and probably evolved as a way to avoid pursuing predators.

Breeding

The breeding season, or rut, begins in mid-November. By this time, both sexes have lost their red summer coat and the antlers of the bucks are ready for action. Mature males have become belligerent and their physical appearance has changed. Not only is the soft velvet gone from their antlers, but the increase in the level of male hormones causes the front shoulders and neck of the bucks to swell. Their frontal appearance is exaggerated, and this helps discourage potential antagonists from combat. Apparently, breeding bucks move through areas occupied by receptive does, breed, and then move on to another group of does. While males will fight for the breeding rights, many tactics are used to avoid combat. Bucks use a variety of visual displays that serve to show off their size and strength. These tactics include a stiff-legged gait, laying the ears along side the neck (accentuates the size of the antlers), and mock battles with bushes and shrubs. Mule deer are not as vocal as elk, but do whine and grunt during the rut. The rut is completed by mid-December.

Gestation is approximately 200 days, with twin fawns born at about 2.7 kg (6 pounds) each. Does usually breed as two year olds and produce spotted, precocial fawns. The doe will hide her fawns in sheltered spots, returning only to allow them to nurse. Hikers will frequently find "abandoned" fawns and, since the female is not immediately present, will rescue the fawn from certain death. However, almost certainly the doe is nearby and the fawn is not abandoned. Never "rescue" any young wildlife unless you are certain the mother is dead. By the time the fawns are three to four weeks old they accompany their mother throughout her spring range. Fawns weigh about 18 kg (40 pounds) when they are weaned in September.

Habits and Habitats

Mule deer range from Minnesota to central Texas, west to the Pacific coast, and from the southern Yukon to central Mexico. Mule deer are characteristic of brushy habitats and are found along streams, canyons, in sagebrush steppe and alpine tundra.

Mule deer were historically categorized as browsers, consuming primarily shrubs. Recent studies have shown that deer will graze on succulent grasses and forbs, therefore, they cannot be considered solely browsers. The rumen of mule deer is fairly small in proportion the their body size; their nutritional strategy is to find and consume the most nutritionally concentrated packets of forage. These concentrated packets are found in the current growth of shrubs and the succulent portions of grasses and forbs. Mule deer attempt to digest their forage as quickly as possible and then excrete it to make room for new material. This strategy ties mule deer to the brushy habitat types and makes them especially vulnerable to poor quality forages.

Mule deer are migratory, moving up to 64 km (40 miles) between summer and winter ranges. Bachelor groups of adolescent and mature bucks usually spend the summers on the alpine, especially in close proximity of the krumholtz woodland. Does usually move up to summer ranges later than bucks since they are responsible for the young. Does with fawns will spend the summer along forest edges or at timber line. Early autumn snows push deer downward to the sagebrush steppe, canyons, or foothills to winter and breed. Mule deer depend on shrubs to successfully over-winter and can effectively use sagebrush, mountain mahogany, and bitter-brush. However, habitats dominated by greasewood and rabbitbrush provide little browse for mule deer.

Lack of adequate winter range seriously constrains mule deer populations in the central Rockies. Ski areas, subdivisions, and reservoirs have all usurped or blocked access to important winter areas. In many areas, mule deer are forced to winter at the top of their winter range rather than the bottom. The end result is that winter survival of mule deer is reduced; starvation, highway collisions, and free-roaming dogs all take their toll.

A strong, viable deer herd will support a large number of predators. Predators from coyotes to mountain lions (and formerly wolves) all prey on deer herds in the central Rockies. Mule deer are also a favorite quarry of human hunters throughout the west. Mule deer have very acute senses of smell and hearing and can easily spot a moving object. However, a stationary object may receive little attention. Primarily nocturnal, mule deer may be observed in the early mornings and late evenings.

Locations

Mule deer are distributed across the state of Colorado, although the greatest concentrations are found west of Interstate 25. On the prairies, mule deer are found along streams, breaks, and canyons. The best winter habitats are found in association with piñon-juniper and ponderosa pine woodlands or mountain shrub communities. Particularly good areas for mule deer are: North Park, Middle Park, Piceance Basin, Gunnison Basin, and the southwestern portion of the state.

Rocky Mountain National Park:

Summer:	Winter:
Forest Canyon Overlook	Fall River Entrance
Below Alpine Visitors Center	Deer Ridge
	Deer Mountain
Gore Range Overlook	Hollowell Park
Medicine Bow Curve	Beaver Meadows Entrance
Upper Kawuneeche Valley	Beaver Meadows

Florissant Fossil Beds National Monument:

Eastern Hornbek Wildlife Loop Trail
Hans Loop Trail
Sawmill Trail

Great Sand Dunes National Monument:

Piñon-juniper woodland along eastern flank of monument
Piñon Flats Campground
Mosca Pass Trail

Special note: Please do not feed any wild animals, especially the deer at Great Sand Dunes.

Mule deer are also visible at Black Canyon, Dinosaur, and Colorado National Monuments and Mesa Verde National Park.

Rocky Mountain Elk
(Cervus elaphus nelsoni)

Elk are the largest round-horned deer in the world. Their near relative, European Red Deer, although smaller, once was considered a separate species. However, recent studies have shown that red deer and elk matings produce fertile offspring. Therefore, these two large types of deer are considered a single Holarctic species and red deer are classified under the scientific name *Cervus elaphus elaphus*. Most readers are familiar with the red deer stag used as a symbol for a national insurance company.

The common name "elk" was misapplied to this animal by early European settlers. In Europe, "elk" is the term used for what we call moose; therefore, early settlers referred to both ungulates as elk. A more appropriate common name for American elk is wapiti, which was the word used by Native Americans for elk. Many authors have tried to convince the public to adopt the usage of wapiti. However, the term elk is so ingrained into the public's mind that its use will probably never cease. All western game and fish agencies sell elk hunting licenses, not wapiti licenses.

Mature bulls stand 135-150 cm (4.5-5 feet) at the shoulder and may weigh in excess of 340 kg (750 pounds). Females are about one-fourth smaller. The bulls grow antlers after their first year, the cows possess none. Yearling bulls develop spike antlers, while adolescents sport antlers with three or four points on a side. A mature bull may grow antlers with a main beam that is 150 cm (5 feet) long and sports six or seven points on a side. The world record elk was taken near Crested Butte, Colorado.

During summer elk are reddish brown on the sides with a chestnut-colored mane and a yellowish-white rump patch. The rump patch is fairly large, the tail is small and yellowish white. Elk begin to grow their winter coats in August, and they are usually complete by the rut. The winter pelage is a darker grey-brown along the sides, and the mane and rump patch maintain their respective colors. The winter coats of mature bulls are noticeably blonde along the sides, and animals can occasionally be sexed from a distance by the color of their winter pelt. However, coats of both sexes bleach during the winter and may be indistinguishable by early spring. Finally, elk possess rudimentary upper canine teeth; they are the only North American deer that have retained their canines. One must be very close to elk to observe these canines, for they are short and well concealed. These canines, or "ivories," were once highly prized by collectors, and that led to the destruction of entire herds during the late 1800s.

Sign

Elk scat has a different appearance during late spring and summer than the balance of the year. Succulent spring and summer forages produce fecal patties similar to those of domestic cattle, but smaller. As forages cure in the fall and winter, fecal pellets are produced which are about 2.5 cm (1 inch) in length. These pellets also show a nipple on one end and a dimple at the other. Fresh elk pellets are usually shiny and black, but turn a dull brown with age.

Elk tracks are broader and less heart shaped than mule deer and considerably larger. The dew claws frequently register in snow and elk tend to drag the tips of their hooves in deep snow, revealing the direction of movement. Elk tracks average 11 x 7 cm (4.3 x 3 inches), especially astute observers can differentiate the slightly larger tracks of bulls from cows.

Elk also leave other indications of their presence. During the rut, bulls will tear at moist ground and thereby dig wallows. They may horn large trees to rid their antlers of velvet or as a visual display to other bulls. Elk also strip the bark off aspen. They hook their lower incisors under the bark and pull up, peeling off the bark. This stripping of bark from aspen weakens the trees and can lead to their death. Winter ranges in Rocky Mountain National Park can easily be spotted because all of the aspen have been barked as high as the elk can reach. Most aspen groves on the eastern side of the park are decadent and dying due to elk over-use.

Breeding

The mating ritual of elk has been the subject of many popular articles and films and is a great drawing card for the western National Parks in autumn. A visitor may witness visual, olfactory, and auditory displays by breeding bulls or even combat over harems of females.

By late August, the antlers of mature males have hardened and the velvet stripped away. Bulls may still tolerate each other's presence, but soon will be found near small herds of cows and calves. In September the rut is well under way, with bulls actively defending harems of cows. A variety of displays are used both by harem and peripheral bulls to attract attention to themselves and show off their size and strength. These displays serve an important function in attempting to avoid combat because fights over females can result in serious injuries. Therefore, bulls use these displays to show off their stature and thus discourage rivals from actively competing for females.

Bugling of the bulls is probably the best known rutting display. Bugling is used to alert potential rivals that a breeding bull is nearby and perhaps to assert their dominance over the cows. The bugle begins as a deep resonating roar, which quickly changes to a shrill whistle and then ends in a series of grunts. Bulls also call attention to themselves by showing off their swollen front shoulders and necks, horning bushes and trees, and digging wallows. Wallowing activities also provide olfactory notice that a breeding bull is a very nasty fellow to deal with, for bulls will urinate and defecate in the wallow before they lay down and roll in it. The bulls attempt to maintain control of their harems both by driving off rivals and actively keeping stray cows with the herd. These activities, in addition to breeding responsibilities, leave little time for feeding, and by the time the rut has ended (usually early November), the breeding bulls have lost a tremendous amount of weight and are exhausted. Large bulls shed their antlers in early March, only yearlings possess their old antlers by May.

Viewing of elk is so popular that Rocky Mountain National Park has restricted visitor activity in the Horseshoe Park meadows during the rut. The Park Service encourages public viewing, but no one is permitted off the main roads in Horseshoe Park. Both spot lighting and use of artificial bugles are also prohibited. Adherence to these regulations allows thousands of visitors to observe the annual breeding ritual of elk in Rocky Mountain.

Single calves are born to the cows about 250 days after breeding. Cows usually begin to calve at the upper portion of their winter range about June 1. The calves weigh about 14 kg (30 pounds) at birth and are reddish with a few small spots. Initially, calves remain hidden while their mothers forage, but within a few weeks they join their mothers with other cows and calves as they move to summer ranges. The calves have been weaned and have developed their winter coats by September. At weaning calves weigh about 100 kg (220 pounds) and attempt to avoid breeding bulls during the rut. Cows usually breed as yearlings and calve every year thereafter. Bulls must attain sufficient size to become socially dominant and may not breed until they are four or five years old.

Habits and Habitats

Historically, elk had the widest distribution of any North American cervid. With the exception of the Great Basin and southeastern coastal plains, they were found from the Atlantic to the Pacific and from northern Alberta into Mexico. Elk were originally animals of open country, especially the

Great Plains, and they were not hesitant to flee into rough or heavily timbered areas to escape danger. This tactic allowed elk to survive the onslaught of European man by retreating into the more inhospitable portions of the Rocky Mountains. By the early 1800s, elk had disappeared from the eastern portion of the continent. The western herds suffered a drastic decline due to market hunting and severe habitat destruction and existed in only a few isolated locations by 1900. Reintroductions (primarily from Yellowstone National Park) re-established herds in the western U.S. Viable elk populations are now found throughout the Rocky Mountains and the Cascades in the U.S. and Canada.

Elk successfully inhabit all forested communities in the central Rockies. Forested habitats are even more valuable to elk if they are near medium-sized montane meadows, alpine tundra, or sagebrush steppe. Elk will feed in the more open areas at night and retreat to the cover of the forest during the day. Elk still retain some of the behavioral attributes of plains animals. Specifically, the females, yearlings, and calves congregate in small herds during the summer and in large herds which may even include mature bulls during the winter. Herding behavior is a characteristic predator protection tactic used by animals across the plains of Africa and America. The senses of the entire group are used to spot danger and alert all herd members.

As one might expect, since elk evolved as animals of open country, they are primarily grazers. That is, they consume mostly grasses along with forbs. Because they are grazers, elk can consume relatively large amounts of poor-quality forage. An elk has a relatively large rumen and can nutritionally afford the long time it takes to digest winter forages. Although an elk cannot speed up the rate of digestion, its rumen is large enough to permit a great amount of digestion to occur per unit time. Therefore, elk can successfully occupy some habitats that are only marginally optimal for other ungulates, e.g. mule deer. Although primarily grazers, elk do not restrict themselves to grasses, but will also utilize shrubs, especially during

winter. Although more difficult to digest than grasses, winter shrubs contain more protein and other nutrients than do grasses. Therefore, it behooves elk to mix shrubs into their diet.

Elk are migratory, moving between distinct summer and winter ranges. During summer, elk occupy montane meadows along timbered edges, krumholtz woodlands, and alpine tundra. Winter elk habitats include: lower montane woodland, low montane meadows, piñon-juniper woodlands, sagebrush and mountain shrub communities. Aspen woodlands are utilized during winter and spring. Some elk in expanding populations may remain in upper winter habitats during the summer.

Elk can tolerate significantly greater snow depths than can deer and occupy winter ranges unsuitable for deer. However, elk cannot tolerate the summer sun and accompanying warm temperatures as well as they can winter temperatures. Therefore, elk will retreat to the cool shade of subalpine forests and other cool areas during summer days. These forests also provide abundant water and seclusion, also important habitat requirements. Elk require areas relatively free from disturbances and will try their best to avoid roads, logging operations, mountain subdivisions, and human activities in general.

Elk are primarily nocturnal, but can be easily observed in most federal parks in the west. Historic predators (bears, wolves, and mountain lions) have sharpened all senses in elk. They probably have the keenest combination of senses of any native ungulate and are exceptionally wise to a stalking human. All of these attributes make close observation difficult, and their skills are continually sharpened, for elk are legally hunted throughout the Rocky Mountain west.

Locations

In Colorado, elk are found in the mountainous portion of the state west of Interstate 25. Colorado probably has one of the largest elk herds in the U.S.; however, elk herds are continually faced with disappearing habitat. Mines, reservoirs, and second-home development have all usurped large portions of elk winter range and blocked historical migration routes. Ski areas frequently occupy both elk winter ranges and calving areas. The result is that more elk are forced onto more marginal winter and calving areas. If we are to maintain our elk herds, elk and other wildlife species must also be considered valuable resources, resources that require our attention and lands free from development.

Although elk are found in all National Forests in Colorado, populations are probably larger west of the Continental Divide. Particularly good areas are North Park, Middle Park, Routt National Forest, White River Plateau, Gunnison Basin, San Juan Mountains, Upper Rio Grande, and the Uncompaghre Plateau.

Rocky Mountain National Park:

Winter:	Summer:
Horseshoe Park	All alpine areas
Beaver Meadows	(especially along
Moraine Park	Trail Ridge Road)
Deer Ridge	Upper Fall River
Beaver Meadows Entrance	Road (Willow Park,
Hidden Valley	Chapin Pass)
Hollowell Park	Cirque below Lava
Burns above Fall River	Cliffs
Lumpy Ridge	Iceberg Pass
Sprague Lake	Gore Range
Estes Park Golf Course	Overlook
	Medicine Bow
	Curve
	Milner Pass
	Specimen Mountain
	Upper Kawuneeche
	Valley

Rutting locations:

Early:	Late:
Upper Fall River Road	Beaver Meadows
Gore Range Overlook	Horseshoe Park
Medicine Bow Curve	Hidden Valley
Specimen Mountain	

Florissant Fossil Beds National Monument:

Along Cave Trail
South of Sawmill Trail
North of Hornbek Wildlife Loop
Northern portion of Monument

Great Sand Dunes National Monument. Although elk are found throughout the Sangre de Cristo Mountains, they are observed in the vicinity of this monument only during winter and spring. Look for elk and their sign in the piñon-juniper and aspen woodlands along the eastern edge of the monument.

Moose *(Alces alces shirasi)*

Moose are the largest cervids in the world. There are currently seven subspecies recognized worldwide, four of which occur in North America. The largest subspecies occurs in Alaska and western Canada. The Shiras, or Wyoming subspecies, inhabits the central and northern Rockies into southern Alberta and British Columbia.

Moose stand 150-185 cm (5-6 feet) at the shoulder. Males average 500 kg (1100 pounds) and females 320 kg (700 pounds). Pelage is a very dark brown and there is no rump patch. Under poor light, moose appear black. The legs and belly are a light tan and the lower legs may be very light, which gives the appearance of stockings. The hair is long and coarse, particularly on the front shoulders and hump. The front legs are longer than the back legs, which accentuates the size of the shoulder hump. The tail is small and inconspicuous, but the head is massive, with a broad muzzle and heavy nose. A flap of skin, called a "bell," hangs from the throat and is usually very long when the animals are young. Bells tend to decrease in length with age. The males have large, flattened (palmate) antlers, and the females have no antlers. Bulls follow the same annual cycle in growing and shedding of antlers as do other cervids. However, large bulls begin to polish the velvet in early September and start to shed antlers by early December. Moose calves are reddish brown when young, yet attain adult coloration by September.

Sign

Moose defecate a fecal pat, similar to elk but larger, when they feed on aquatic plants

44

or succulent vegetation. Winter scat is pelleted, more oblong than elk pellets, and both ends are rounded. Pellets average 4 cm (1.5 inches) and may be very pale and appear to be composed of saw dust when the moose is feeding on browse.

Moose tracks are larger than an elk's, more pointed, and the dew claws register more often. Adults leave tracks 15 x 10 cm (6 x 4 inches), and the stride averages 120-150 cm (4-5 feet). Moose also leave evidence of their activities by wallows, scarred trees, and highlining willows.

Breeding

Moose breed from mid September into November. The bulls do not gather harems of cows; rather, bulls will stay with one cow, defend his rights to her, breed her, and then move on to another cow. Moose are solitary animals, and their rutting behavior reflects their solitary nature. Bulls will emit a deep grunt-like call during the rut and are very aggressive towards any intruder—moose or human.

Cows give birth usually to a single calf, but occasionally to twins, from mid-May to early June. The calves are not spotted, but are simply a smaller, reddish version of the adult. A cow is very aggressive in defense of her young and is probably no less dangerous than a sow bear with cubs. This fierce nature is important because the lone cow must drive away any potential predator (wolves, bears, and lions). However, calves are weaned in six months, and then the cow turns all her fury towards her offspring. The cow must displace her calf far from her turf so that they will not compete with each other for habitat resources.

Habits and Habitats

Moose are animals of northern, boreal forests and lakes. Moose are a solitary, colonizing specie that effectively exploit new openings in or at the edge of forests. Their distribution is limited by hot, dry areas, lack of browse on the tundra, and in some areas by disease. Moose use areas where the mature climax forest has been disturbed by fires, floods, glaciers, avalanches, or plant diseases. Since these openings are fairly small and widely distributed, they cannot be successfully utilized by herds of large herbivores, but rather supply sufficient food only for solitary animals. Habitat characteristics are what force moose to be great wanderers and why cows so fiercely drive their calves away at weaning. Individual animals must find unoccupied pockets of moose habitat that can support them and still be near enough to other moose to allow successful breeding.

Moose are year-round inhabitants of subalpine, lodgepole, and aspen forests and high elevation riparian communities in the central and northern Rockies. Although moose have seasonal ranges, their migrations are short compared to the other cervids discussed here. Moose can withstand severe winter temperatures and relatively deep snow. These abilities permit them to winter higher than other ungulates. Willow bottoms are very important to moose during winter. The single most important characteristic of moose habitat is a plentiful supply of water. The forages consumed by moose are found in very moist sites and even under water.

Moose are perhaps the most primitive of all North American ruminants. Plant digestibility is related in a general way to moisture content, the more succulent the forage, the more digestible. Moose rely on aquatic vegetation during the summer and feed both along shores and below the surface of lakes and ponds. Even willows, which make up the majority of the winter diet, are more digestible than other browse species available on the winter ranges. By foraging on wetland vegetation, moose assure themselves of a good supply of moderately digestible forage which can be processed relatively quickly.

Locations

Although huntable populations of moose exist in Utah and Wyoming, the historical status of moose in Colorado is somewhat speculative. Confirmed moose sightings have

45

occurred since the mid 1860s from western Larimer county to the vicinity of Hayden and Steamboat Springs. Milton Estes killed a moose in Estes Park sometime between 1860 and 1866, and other individuals were killed in the vicinity of Steamboat Springs in the 1940s and 1950s. These individuals were undoubtedly migrants from Wyoming seeking new areas to colonize and were killed before sufficient numbers were attracted to form a viable, breeding population. There is no doubt that Colorado has considerable habitat suitable for moose.

In 1978 and 1979, moose were transplanted into the Illinois River drainage in southern Jackson County. These animals have multiplied significantly despite the annual loss of several individuals to poachers (most animals were shot by elk hunters who misidentified the moose as elk). The Colorado moose have now expanded their range to include other areas in North Park, Middle Park, and even into Summit and Clear Creek Counties. A special hunting season is now held for moose in North Park. Two or three hunters receive permits to hunt moose each November.

Rocky Mountain National Park. Since the moose transplant occurred just outside the western boundary of RMNP, it is not surprising that a few individuals began exploring the western portions of the park. Currently, a small herd has established itself in the Kawuneeche Valley. This small herd probably numbers less than ten and may be encountered throughout the valley during the summer. However, the herd apparently restricts itself to the area between Onahu Creek and Grand Lake during the winter.

Since moose occur only in north-central Colorado currently, they are not found in or near either Florissant Fossil Beds, Great Sand Dunes National Monument, or any other federal park.

Bison *(Bison bison)*

Bison require no detailed description to anyone even marginally familiar with the history of the American West. Bison were intimately connected with the settling of the western frontier. Bison (commonly referred to as buffalo) are the largest terrestrial animal native to North America. Mature bison stand 150-183 cm (5-6 feet) at the shoulders; mature males may weigh in excess of 1000 kg (2200 pounds). Females weigh more than one-third less, or 500-600 kg (1100-1300 pounds). Bison are dark brown with long, shaggy, dark fur over the head, front shoulders and front legs which is distinct from the short, smooth, light brown coat that extends over the hindquarters. The tail is moderately long with a tuft of big, black hairs on the tip. The head is massive, and long hair extends over the throat to produce a beard. Both sexes have true horns which are short, black, and gently curve upward. The head and horns of the bulls is generally much more massive than the cow's. Calves are reddish when first born, but molt into a more adult-like pelage by October.

Sign

Bison scat appears virtually identical to that of range cattle, although it is usually drier and somewhat smaller than cattle's scat. On a dry diet bison will leave a layered scat that is quite distinctive. Dried bison chips were used by both Indians and early settlers as a fuel source for fires on the Great Plains.

Bison tracks generally resemble those of range cattle, but are slightly more round. The tips of the hooves are pointed and the backs are rounded. On very hard surfaces, individual hooves do not register and a single rounded track, resembling a horse track, may result. Tracks average 15 x 16 cm (5 x 6 inches) for mature animals.

Bison also leave behind wallowed depressions, usually as the result of dust baths. These dust baths protect from insects, and the wallows are frequently 30 cm (1 foot) deep and can be 300 cm (10 feet) long or longer. Wallows used year after year can leave a long-lasting mark on grasslands. In some areas of virgin prairie, bison wallows over 100 years old can still be easily spotted.

Breeding

Bison breed from mid-July to September; a certain clue is the presence of mature bulls within the cow-calf herds. The sexes usually segregate themselves except during the rut. Bison are promiscuous, and battles between rival bulls are not infrequent. Several fights may be observed simultaneously within the same herd. Cows are usually receptive only for two or three days and may be bred by several bulls during this short time.

Calves are born during May after a 9.5 month gestation period. They are precocial and able to run with the herd after a few days. Some newborn calves may be observed in late summer or early fall. These calves are the result of late breeding and stand little chance of surviving the coming winter.

Bison are sexually mature at four years and most cows breed at this time. However, a bull must attain sufficient size to be socially dominant before he can breed. Most bulls are seven or eight years old before they are socially mature. Theoretically, cows are capable of producing a calf annually; however, this rate of productivity is seldom attained. Range quality and diseases are important constraints on the reproductive potential of bison.

Habits and Habitats

Bison are gregarious animals that depend on grasslands to provide their food. Historically many types of grasslands were utilized; forest openings in the east, alpine tundra, montane meadows in the west, and the prairies of the Great Plains. Historically, bison were found from New York and Pennsylvania to Georgia; across the prairies to the Rockies and west to eastern Oregon and Washington. Bison were also found from northern Mexico to the Yukon. Although it is impossible to determine their historic numbers, the most frequently cited figure is 60 million animals. The highest densities were found in the area between Illinois and Idaho and from north Texas to the Northern Saskatchewan River. This core area was probably inhabited by 30 million bison.

Two subspecies of bison are currently recognized (based on cranial mass), plains bison *(Bison bison bison)* and wood bison *(Bison bison athabascae)*. Plains bison ranged throughout the eastern U.S. and the Great Plains, while wood bison were found from the Rockies in Colorado and Utah north into Canada. Introduction of plains bison to the native wood bison herd at Wood Buffalo National Park apparently doomed the last chance of maintaining a pure wood bison herd. However, in the late 1950s, biologists discovered an isolated herd of bison at Wood Buffalo National Park. After confirmation that this was indeed a pure wood bison herd, most of the animals were transferred to Elk Island National Park, Alberta, and McKenzie Bison Sanctuary in the Northwest Territories.

Bison are supremely adapted to life in open country. They consume most forages in their path and are not very selective feeders. Recent studies on the Pawnee National Grasslands have shown that bison can efficiently digest low-protein, poor-quality forages. Bison are more efficient in processing these forages than are cattle.

Bison use grasslands extensively, but will retreat to the shelter of forests for shade, to escape insects, and as protection from severe weather. Apparently, wood bison were most effective in utilizing montane meadows; large, intermontane parks and alpine tundra, and plains bison were found on the open prairies. Bison evolved under the severe selection pressures of Pleistocene glaciation and can withstand onslaughts of severe winter weather. Their coats are impervious to the wind-driven chill of the prairies, and they can find forages buried beneath deep snow by simply swinging their heads back and forth, bulldozing the snow aside.

From the herds of millions, bison numbers plummeted during the end of the 19th century. The famous naturalist, William T. Hornaday, censused bison in January, 1889, and was shocked at his discovery. Hornaday counted 200 under supposed federal protection in Yellowstone, 550 near Great Slave Lake, and 256 in scattered zoos and private collections. Hornaday could only account for

85 free-ranging (and therefore unprotected) bison surviving in the United States. Finally, eight years later, poachers killed two bulls, a cow, and a calf in Lost Park, Colorado (Park County), the last wild, unprotected bison in the country.

How had this happened? How could an animal whose numbers had seemed endless have been brought to the verge of extinction by 1900? The answer—war and politics.

Bison were central to the life of the American Indian. Indians hunted bison in a variety of ways and, when successful, used every possible part of the animal for their needs. Food, clothing, utensils, saddles, sleds, ceremonial and religious objects, all were obtained from bison. Soon, the expanding white U.S. population sought to appropriate the Indian lands for themselves. Naturally, the Indians objected, and the infamous Indian wars resulted. The United States government soon learned that it could ill afford a protracted guerilla-type war on its western frontier. An economic decision was made and implemented by General William T. Sherman to starve the Indians into submission by destroying the bison. Sherman blocked legislation designed to protect bison and promoted the bison's destruction by all white soldiers and settlers. This strategy was successful, for the native Americans were brought into total submission after the massacre at Wounded Knee, South Dakota, in 1890. The last wild bison were destroyed in Colorado only a few years later in 1897.

After the destruction of the great bison herds, hunters and tanners were put out of business. These people had made an easy living from the bison. Bison had developed their huge body size as a defense mechanism. Bison had little to fear from a frontal attack by any predator. Consequently, they usually stood their ground and faced the danger head on. This tactic was usually successful against wolves, grizzlies, and even native Americans. However, it was not successful against the buffalo hunter. These hunters could destroy an entire group by killing individuals with a single shot from long range. The herd would not scatter unless the

hunter wounded an animal. Now the buffalo hunter had destroyed his commodity and the only monetary opportunity left was collecting bison bones and shipping them back east to be used as fertilizer and in bone china. Whites and Indians collected bison bones side by side as a way to make money. One rick of bison bones (near Springfield, Colorado) awaiting rail shipment to the east contained an estimated 350,000 cubic feet on bones, enough bones to make about 90,000 bison skeletons.

Today bison exist in a semi-domesticated state in several state and national parks and private ranches. Perhaps there are 30,000 bison in North America today, but the only truly wild herds are found in Utah's Wilson Mountains, Yellowstone National Park, and Wood Buffalo National Park.

Locations

Bison once ranged over the entire state of Colorado, and both subspecies were present. Of course, we know that bison occurred in the eastern plains and mountain parks, but specific locations are based on historical accounts and archeological evidence.

Old bison jumps and traps (Indian kill sites) are located along the north fork of the Cache La Poudre River, in North Park, along the eastern edge of Estes Park, and in numerous sites in eastern Colorado. The review of maps from across the state shows the presence of numerous landmarks named for bison; Buffalo Creek, Buffalo Pass, etc., which were obviously named by pioneers for the animals observed there. Verification that bison used alpine tundra comes from historical accounts of Arapahos hunting bison on Thatchtop Mountain in Rocky Mountain Park. In 1983, two bison skulls were found melting out of glaciers at the headwaters of the Big Thompson River, providing additional evidence that bison utilized the alpine landscape.

Fortunately, the bone hunters did not gather all the bison bones from our prairies. I have found horn sheaths in freshly plowed wheat fields and skulls eroding out of prairie stream banks. We no longer have wild bison roaming Colorado; all that is left are a few bones, which bear stark testament to our unwillingness to share this world with other creatures, man and animal alike.

Bison cannot be observed in any of the federal parks in Colorado, although all areas were certainly inhabited by them. A small herd that formerly inhabited Colorado National Monument has recently been removed by the National Park Service. The Colorado Division of Wildlife formerly classified bison as a game animal and conducted limited hunts on several herds intensively managed by them. However, the bison's need for prodigious amounts of real estate and their indifference to fencing forced the Division of Wildlife to dispose of their herds.

Bison can be observed in Colorado today, but only in small, intensively managed herds. Bison can be viewed at the following locations:

Rawhide Power Plant—along I-25 west of Carr
Genesee Mountain Park—along I-70 west of Denver
Desperation Store—along U.S. 34 east of Kersey
Cunningham Buffalo Ranch—Haxtun
Along Highway 119, south of Central City
La Mesa Buffalo Ranch—Nathrop
Basman Ranch—Calhan
B-J Acres—Longmont
Bijou Creek Buffalo Ranch—Wiggins
Brachtenback Ranch—Stratten
Lazy R.K. Ranch—Parker
Downare Ranch—Hartsel
Herbst Ranch—Kiowa
Colorado Bison Company—Mead
Lay Valley Bison Ranch—Craig
Price Brothers—Sedgewick
High Meadow Buffalo—Center
High Wire Ranch—Steamboat Springs

Rocky Mountain Goat
(Oreamnos americanus)

Mountain goats are not true goats at all, but are more closely related to the antelope of Africa. Their closest relatives are the chamois that inhabit the Alps. Goats are not closely related to any North American specie.

The general public is probably more unfamiliar with mountain goats than any other native big game. Because of their inhospitable habitat, few people ever observe free-roaming mountain goats. Visitors frequently confuse mountain goats with female bighorn sheep.

The mountain goat is a very solidly built, blocky animal with a short tail and distinct shoulder hump. The pelage is white, although on older animals it may be a yellowish, cream color. There appears to be a beard on the chin, but in reality the beard is made up of long hairs hanging from the throat. The ears are fairly long and are pointed. The skull of mountain goats is fairly fragile in contrast to bighorn sheep. Goats possess true horns, which are round and pointed and curve gently backward. Black scent glands lie behind the base of the horns. These glands function to mark vegetation during the rut. The black, pencil-like horns range in size from 21-31 cm (7-12 inches) long and are similar in both sexes. Generally, the horns of the male (billy) are more massive and do not curve as sharply back. Mountain goats stand 90-105 cm (3-3.5 feet) at the shoulder and weigh between 45 and 140 kg (100-310 pounds). Females are about one-fifth smaller than males.

Sign

Mountain goats excrete pellets year around. These pellets are slightly smaller than mule deer pellets and are very difficult to distinguish from bighorn sheep pellets. In general, goat pellets are smaller than sheep pellets and tend to be darker.

The hooves of mountain goats are relatively large for their body size, including the dew claws. These large hooves help the goats to walk on snow with less floundering than other ungulates. The hooves have a horny rim and a soft, sponge-like pad. This arrangement provides excellent traction for mountain goats on the cliffs and rock faces they inhabit. Tracks have a generally square shape with the front tips being splayed and rounded.

A sure sign of mountain goat country is an abundance of long strands of white hair left behind on bushes and rocks. The winter coat starts to molt in June and the goats attempt to accelerate the shedding process by rubbing against any object capable of snagging the hair.

Breeding

Mountain goats breed from early November through mid-December. The breeding system of mountain goats of poorly understood. The nannies appear to control the breeding, only tolerating males when receptive. The nannies do not flee from courting males, but instead fend off the males' advances until the nannies are in season. Goats may be monogamous with one male servicing only one female. Unlike other ungulates, battles between males are not characterized by head-to-head clashes. Their delicate skulls would not withstand the force. Rather, goats stand head to tail and attempt to gore each other along the flanks and stomach. Thick layers of skin, up to 2.3 cm (0.9 inches) thick, protect these areas. Goats bleed very little when punctured due to rapid constriction of the affected vessels and efficient clotting. Mountain goats do occasionally severely injure one another during battles, and some injuries are severe enough to cause death.

Kids are born in late May or early June, about 150 days after mating. Usually nannies give birth to single kids, but in expanding herds, twinning is fairly common. Kids weigh about 3 kg (6.6 pounds) at birth and are white except for their eyes, noses, and hooves The kids are born without horns, but within a few weeks budding horns are visible. Mountain goats gain their balance and climbing ability with amazing speed. Within a few hours of birth kids are exploring the steep cliffs of their isolated nursery. In a few days, a kid can follow its mother virtually throughout her range.

Habits and Habitats

Mountain goats are animals of open, precipitous, high elevation terrain. They feed in the grasslands of the alpine and subalpine zone. During winter, some herds may descend into the subalpine forest to feed in sheltered sites. However, most goat herds spend the winter above timberline on wind-blasted ridges and cliffs where the snow has been swept clear and they can still find adequate forage. Mountain goats inhabit the most inhospitable areas of the continent. Their climbing abilities truly seem incredible, and one can only wonder how they are able to place themselves in some areas. Goats are usually seen from a distance, on a mountain top or in the middle of a cliff face. Getting close to goats once they have been spotted can be an adventure in itself.

Mountain goats historically ranged along the coastal mountains of southern Alaska and British Columbia. Interior mountain ranges of the Yukon and Alberta were also inhabited by goats, as well as the northern mountains of Washington, Idaho, and Montana. Mountain goats were apparently unable to negotiate the high temperatures, lack of water, and gentle terrain in southern Wyoming. This barrier effectively limited mountain goat distribution to northern areas. However, goats have successfully been transplanted into suitable habitats in Wyoming, South Dakota, Oregon, Colorado, and Nevada.

The range of bighorn sheep and mountain goats frequently overlap. Although little is known about the degree of competition between these two species, some important differences do exist. While both groups use climax alpine and subalpine grasslands, goats use more precipitous terrain and generally winter higher than bighorns. Although goats are gregarious, as are bighorns, they do not have the advanced, complex social organization that typifies bighorns. Goats are colonizers, and therefore, they are more independent of the herd than are bighorns.

Goats utilize a wide variety of forages, and this permits them to successfully inhabit many areas with little or no competition. In the central Rockies, goats consume mostly grasses and grass-like plants. However, during winter goats will browse on willows and other woody species as they descend into the subalpine woodlands. Water is not a limiting resource for goats since the alpine has an abundance of water during the summer. Mountain goats will eat snow during the winter as a source of free water.

Mountain goats have few enemies because few predators are able to navigate the precipitous terrain that goats call home. Golden eagles will prey on kids, and wolves have been known to kill goats caught in the open away from escape cover (cliffs, boulder fields, etc.). Mountain lions are probably the most serious threat to goats, since these cats are sufficiently nimble to traverse some parts of goat habitat. However, lions can hunt goats only when the deep snows are gone and, therefore, only rarely prey upon goats.

The habitat that goats live in is the chief factor in determining mortality. Despite their uncanny abilities to defy steep terrain, accidents do occur. Goats slip and fall from high peaks and cliffs, especially when snow and ice coat the rocks and make them slippery. The greatest enemy of mountain goats is the avalanche. A favorite winter abode of goats lies in the cliffs along avalanche chutes. It is not uncommon for an entire group of goats to be caught and buried by an avalanche.

Locations

Mountain goats were successfully introduced into five areas of Colorado between 1948 and 1972. Goats were transplanted from Montana, Idaho, and South Dakota. Goat herds established from these transplants have successfully colonized other areas of suitable habitat and will probably continue to expand into presently unoccupied areas of the state. Currently, mountain goats are classified as a big game animal in Colorado and may be legally hunted. A small number of permits are randomly drawn from a list of annual applicants.

A small herd of mountain goats ranges along the continental divide in the Never Summer Mountains north into the Rawah Wilderness. A herd that supports limited hunting inhabits the Gore Range north of Vail. Probably the most visible goat herd in the continental U.S. can be found in the Mt. Evans area and west to Greys and Toreys Peaks. The Mt. Evans herd was established in 1961 and has grown to sufficient size to support hunting. Visitors who travel the Mt. Evans highway have an excellent opportunity to observe goats. Favored locations along the highway include: cliffs above Lincoln Lake; cliffs behind Summit Lake; and the upper Chicago Creek Basin. Two small goat herds range southwest of Aspen and in the Raggeds Wilderness. The largest goat herd in the state was established in 1948 in the Collegiate Range west of Salida and Buena Vista. Goats now roam throughout the Collegiates and can occasionally be seen by summer visitors along the Cottonwood Pass highway. The remaining herd of mountain goats lives in the remote San Juan Mountains east of the Animas River between Silverton and Durango. This herd is centered about the West Needles Mountains in Chicago Basin and is difficult to access.

Rocky Mountain National Park. Mountain goats are infrequently seen in the Never Summer Mountains along the west boundary of RMNP. This herd is very small and wanders throughout these mountains. Mountain goats are not found in any other federal park in Colorado.

Bighorn Sheep *(Ovis canadensis)*

The exploits of bighorn sheep and the spectacular mountain ranges inhabited by them have been the subject of many popular articles and films. For most people, these glimpses of bighorn life and their habitats are all the experience they will ever have with bighorns. Bighorns certainly do inhabit spectacular wilderness areas across the Rockies, yet bighorns are readily observable to those intent on seeing them. Bighorns are herbivores that depend on acute vision and open, rough terrain to avoid danger. These rough habitats are available both in the high mountains and along river canyons, and bighorns are found in both areas.

There is significant sexual dimorphism in bighorn sheep, i.e. there are many obvious differences between males and females. So significant is the sexual dimorphism in bighorns that each sex will be discussed separately.

Rams are blocky animals with massive front shoulders and deep chests. Adult rams stand 106 cm (3.5 feet) at the shoulder and may weigh as much as 160 kg (350 pounds). The heads of mature rams sport large brown or amber colored horns. These are true horns and grow continuously throughout the sheep's life. Annual rings are laid down and can be used to age sheep. The horns taper along their length and generally form a backward "C" shape about the ram's head. If the ram lives long enough and highly nutritious forages are present, the horns will the complete the arc and form a full curl. Pelage colors of bighorns vary over their range. Sheep are light brown or gray in desert areas, but are a rich, dark brown in the Rockies. This dark brown pelage contrasts sharply with the large, white rump patch. There is a black stripe down the center of the rump patch which ends with the short black tail. The dark brown color is most noticeable when sheep molt into their winter coat. However, this coat soon is bleached by the winter sun, and by spring, sheep may appear almost white because of the bleaching process.

Female bighorns are more slender than rams and, in fact, resemble an adolescent male whose growth and maturity has been arrested. Ewes average 65 kg (143 pounds) and stand about 90 cm (3 feet) at the shoulder. Although the general pattern of coloration is the same as rams, the patterns are not as distinct in ewes. Ewes have short, spike-like horns that curve slightly backward. Although ewes generally outlive males, horns from ewes infrequently exceed 26 cm (10 inches). It is very easy to confuse young males with mature ewes. I will discuss the social significance of this observation later.

Sheep are gregarious animals with a highly evolved, complex social system. Lone sheep are almost never encountered, for they are not an adventuresome, colonizing species. The intricacies of sheep behavior have served to successfully perpetuate this animal, however, the rapid alterations of sheep habitat by man has turned some aspects of sheep behavior against them.

Sign

Bighorn scat generally resembles both mule deer and mountain goat pellets. The pellets are about 1 cm (0.4 inches) and so are larger than mountain goat pellets. Sheep pellets tend to have a nipple-like projection on one end and a flattened bottom. Probably the best clue to bighorn pellets is an abundance of pellets in a bedding area. Bighorns use favorite spots habitually. After a bed ground is used year after year, the area is covered with pellets. The beds are usually in rocky areas or at the top of cliffs and are a shallow, oval-shaped depression about 120 cm (4 feet) long.

Bighorn tracks generally resemble mule deer tracks, but are wedge shaped rather than heart shaped. The front tips are not pointed, but are squared off. The edges are straight and the entire track is more blocky than a deer's track. Sheep tracks average 9 x 6.5 cm (3.5 x 2.5 inches). The soles of a bighorn hoof are soft and crescent shaped. Occasionally, a perfect track will show the raised, crescent outline of the sole.

Winter and early spring ranges frequently will retain evidence of shed winter coats. Unlike the long, copious white hair characteristic of mountain goats, shed bighorn hair is usually found in patches. The hair of bighorns is not as long and wooly as mountain goat hair and is more brittle. Therefore, one usually finds small patches of sheep hair on rocks and on the ground of winter and spring ranges.

Breeding

Bighorns breed from mid-November through late December. Although bighorns have developed a complex social system, their rutting behavior appears anything but organized. To understand sheep breeding, we must take a brief look at general sheep behavior.

Adult ewes and adult rams are easily distinguished from one another, while juvenile rams only begin to resemble adult rams when they are five to six years old. These recognition factors are the keys to understanding sheep behavior. Mature rams also have difficulty telling adult ewes and juvenile rams apart. Therefore, the rams treat all sheep smaller than themselves as females and socially dominate them. Dominant rams will display and court females and young rams alike. Dominant rams will even mount young rams, and the subordinate rams will stand for them. Naturally, when the females are in heat, the majority of courting displays are directed toward the ewes.

Unlike other ungulates, sheep constantly test each other's social rank and are intensely active behaviorally all year. When one ram displays and courts another ram, he insults the subordinate. As long as the dominant ram is larger, the younger ram will tolerate the insults. However, if both rams are of equal size or if the insulted ram is the larger, a spectacular dominance fight will follow. The rams may kick one another and attempt to mount. Finally, they will back off a short distance, rise to their back legs, cock their heads, and fall forward, propelling their horns together with a mighty crack that can be heard up to 1.6 km (1 mile) away. The rams may fight in this manner for a few minutes or several hours. Occasionally, the rams will injure one another, but more frequently they simply exhaust themselves and the weaker ram withdraws from the battle. Ewes also fight and butt one another, especially when a favorite resource (e.g. salt) is in short supply. However, their battles are not so dramatic or long lasting.

As a young ram grows up, he constantly tests himself and his social position until he attains the size and strength necessary to displace his elders. After a ram reaches social maturity, his days are numbered. The constant stress of maintaining his social position soon drains him and he may only live for another three or four years.

When the breeding season arrives, the bands of rams join the ewe groups on the rutting grounds. The rams defend no territories or harems of females. Rather, they will gather around a ewe that is about to cycle or already in heat. The rams will test her urine and approach her with their heads low and cocked to one side. Usually, the ewe will run away and the rams will chase her, butt each other, and push each other aside. It is not unusual for four or five rams to gather around a single ewe, court her, and fight each other. Frequently, while two rams are preoccupied fighting each other, a third ram will sneak up to the ewe and breed her. In this fashion, the ewe may be bred several times by several rams during her short heat cycle. The breeding system of bighorns can, therefore, be best described as chaotic. Several rams will surround a ewe, court her, chase her, battle over her, finally breed her, and then move on to the next ewe in heat. This system is energetically draining on both males and females, because the ewes are hassled and harried by numerous rams and flee their advances until receptive. The result is that both breeding males and females are somewhat fatigued by the end of the rut. As with other ungulates, the rams have expended abundant energy and spent little time feeding, resulting in almost total exhaustion.

Bighorn lambs are born 180 days after conception in a very secluded, precipitous lambing area. Lambs are born from mid-May into June, weigh about 3 kg (6.5 pounds), and generally resemble their mothers in coloration. Within a few days the lamb has attained remarkable climbing abilities and follows its mother from the nursery to its summer home. The lamb grows quickly and may weigh 30 kg (65 pounds) by weaning in the fall. A single lamb is born to the ewe, twinning is extremely rare. The first year of life is the most important for the survival of the lamb. Predators, disease, and exposure are all important mortality factors. The ewe does not drive the lamb away from her at weaning. A ewe lamb will be absorbed into the female group, a ram lamb will stay with ewes until he is about two, then he will join the adult rams.

Bighorns have the lowest reproductive potential of all native ungulates. Females first breed at 2.5 years, but rams do not breed until socially mature, at about seven or eight years. Lambs are born into a severe spring environment and many do not survive, further reducing production. The low productivity of bighorns is not a disadvantage to this slow maturing, socially complex species, because they exploit stable, climax communities. Low production is a liability to sheep in a world characterized by severe, sudden habitat changes.

Habits and Habitats

Bighorns once roamed the mountains and canyons of the west from Alberta and British Columbia to Baja, California, and northern Mexico. Their eastern distribution was limited to the badlands of North and South Dakota and the canyons of west Texas. In the far west they inhabited the Cascades and Sierra Nevadas. Present-day bighorn distribution is a very small proportion of that historic range. One subspecies, the badlands bighorn, is extinct. Bighorn numbers were reduced by extensive market hunting, habitat destruction, competition with domestic livestock, and disease.

Sheep feed primarily on grasses and grass-like plants, although some browse is consumed, especially during winter. Bighorns still occupy climax grasslands of the alpine and subalpine. Some herds utilize grasslands associated with river canyons throughout the year. However, the principal component common in each of these communities is readily available escape cover, cliffs, steep slopes, or talus slopes.

Bighorns evolved in the wide open, productive grasslands that developed upon the retreat of Pleistocene glaciers. These sheep developed anti-predator strategies based on visual location of the enemy and escape to rough, rocky, precipitous terrain that precluded pursuit by most predators. Wolves were occasionally able to catch bighorns caught far from escape cover and bears also rarely took sheep. Golden eagles and mountain lions were and probably still are the most successful predators of bighorns.

The open grasslands that developed in the wake of glaciers provided the forage, terrain, and visibility necessary to ensure viable sheep populations. Populations grew and gradually expanded across the continent, principally because few visual barriers to sheep movement existed. Sheep were able to cross open country, staying near escape cover, and not increase their vulnerability to predators. While sheep used favorite feeding and bedding areas routinely, there was sufficient habitat to prevent overcrowding. Additionally, sheep were able to exploit distinct winter and summer ranges, as well as migration routes between seasonal ranges.

As the forests gradually invaded the open grasslands, the ability of sheep to colonize new areas declined. However, bighorns continued their winter-summer migrations, even through stands of timber. Bighorns were able to migrate through timber because adults knew the routes between winter and summer ranges and taught the younger sheep the way.

The entire behavioral-migratory system was disrupted when the whites began to settle the west. Initially, bighorns were over hunted, many on winter ranges where they were a concentrated, easy prey for men with rifles. Sheep soon learned to avoid these wintering areas and attempted to winter in higher, more remote country. Fire suppression activities allowed bighorn habitat to become overgrown with brush and timber, and that led to avoidance of these areas by sheep. The ultimate effect of these activities served to concentrate sheep on remote, marginal pieces of habitat. Sheep herds lost the knowledge of migration routes to their winter ranges, and the increase in forests kept them from colonizing new areas. Sheep numbers declined because marginal winter areas were unable to support high numbers of sheep and the concentrations of sheep at bedding and feeding sites spread diseases throughout entire herds.

Domestic livestock also invaded sheep habitat and exposed sheep to new diseases, removed forage, and forced them into even smaller parcels of habitat. The livestock diseases devastated many herds and the unnatural concentrations of sheep promoted heavy infestations of a natural sheep parasite—the lungworm. Sheep infect themselves with lungworm when they accidentally ingest small snails along with their forage. The snails are infected with the worms and worms migrate from the sheep's digestive tract to its lungs, where they reproduce. The worm's eggs are coughed up and swallowed by the sheep and are excreted in the feces. Snails feed on the fecal pellets, become infected with the lungworm, and the cycle starts again. Most adults can withstand a moderate number of lungworms. However, a heavy parasite load predisposes adults to pneumonia, from which they cannot recover. Additionally, lungworms from a pregnant ewe will cross the placenta and infect the unborn lamb. Lambs are then born with a very heavy parasite load, develop pneumonia, and usually die before fall. Bighorn populations have been subject to extensive die-offs since their habitats were altered by man.

Current management schemes attempting to restore bighorn numbers stress habitat development and treatment of diseases. Timbered areas near sheep ranges are burned to open them up and encourage sheep use. Burning not only provides open habitat for bighorns, but also stimulates nutritious forages used by sheep. Sheep have been transplanted into some areas to re-establish historic herds or at low elevation winter ranges adjacent to existing herds. This latter tactic encourages the transplanted herd to become familiar with a winter range, then make contact with the resident herd at higher elevations during the summer. Then, the transplanted sheep lead some of the residents to the new winter range, thus establishing a migration route between high summer range and a low elevation winter range. This technique has been successful in Rocky Mountain National Park. Livestock grazing in sheep ranges has been reduced or eliminated, thereby reducing competition for forage and risk of disease transmission from livestock to bighorns. Finally, some sheep herds are treated during the late winter with drugs that kill lungworm. The goal is to kill lungworms in the adult ewe before they migrate into the fetus. This technique has been successful and has helped to increase sheep herds throughout the central Rockies.

Unfortunately, some bighorn herds are continuing to experience loss of habitat because of human encroachment. Some of the most productive herds live at least part of their lives in river canyons. Many reservoirs have been built or are proposed for these river canyons. The result is loss of very productive winter habitat and the decline of the herd. Bighorns require some portion of their ranges free of human disturbance. Ski areas, logging operations, and increased back country travel have all decreased the value of habitat to support bighorns.

As a token of the high esteem with which Colorado residents regard bighorns, the state legislature designated the bighorn as Colorado's official state animal in 1961. A bighorn ram is used as the symbol of the Colorado Division of Wildlife and the Colorado Wildlife Federation. The bighorn is also the unofficial symbol of Rocky Mountain National Park. Currently, bighorn are classified as big game in Colorado and may be legally hunted. Hunters receive their licenses in a lottery-type drawing and must take a ram of specified size.

Locations

Bighorns have been re-established in historic ranges across Colorado. However, most herds exist in isolated, island-type habitats; sheep distribution is not as continuous as in pristine times. Desert bighorns have been transplanted to canyons around

Colorado National Monument and the lower Dolores River Canyon. However, no tangible evidence exists that desert bighorn ever inhabited Colorado. Bighorns formerly inhabited those areas into which desert bighorns were transplanted, but they were undoubtedly Rocky Mountain Bighorns.

Generally, bighorns range over most alpine areas of Colorado, some river canyons along the front range and western border, and even in canyons stretching out into the southeastern prairies. Usually, the most productive herds are those that summer in the alpine and winter along canyons or low-elevation badlands. Many relict herds exist that must live summer and winter on the alpine. These herds are stable, but are vulnerable to elimination by a single disease outbreak or catastrophic winter. The largest, most productive, and most viable herds are listed below, but this list must not be considered totally exhaustive.

A special note is mandatory at this time. Bighorns are a very sensitive, nervous species. If you are fortunate enough to observe sheep, please do not chase and harass the bighorns. Watch from a distance or from your car. If you discover sheep along the trail, simply sit down and wait for them to approach you. Bighorns are curious and may come towards you. If you harass the sheep, you may jeopardize their health, because they are subject to anaphylactic reactions.

Bighorns roam the Yampa River Canyon west of Maybell, near Cross Mountain. A herd of bighorns is scattered throughout the Never Summer Mountains and the Rawah Wilderness.

One of the most visible sheep herds in the state lives along the north rim of the Cache la Poudre Canyon. One herd lives in the "Narrows" and another upstream from Indian Meadows to Poudre Falls. These herds are especially visible during winter along Highway 14.

Winter visitors frequently observe bighorns along Interstate 70 near Georgetown or above Empire. Another visible herd spends the summer along the Mt. Evans highway. During the 1950s, the largest bighorn herd in the U.S. inhabited the Kenosha and Tarryall Mountains. A severe pneumonia epidemic severely reduced this herd, but both ranges are still inhabited by bighorns.

Bighorns range north of Woodland Park in the Rampart Range. This herd has produced the top trophy heads for North American bow hunters. Sheep also live on Pikes Peak and can be seen both from the highway and cog railway during the summer. The range of the Pikes Peak herd extends south along Beaver Creek towards Penrose. Sheep also range along the Arkansas River from Canyon City to Buena Vista, in the Collegiate Range and in the Mosquito Range.

Formerly, a viable bighorn herd occupied the Gore Range north of Vail, but development of the ski area, land use conversions, and the increased human density all have negatively affected this herd.

Huntable populations of bighorns are found in the Wet Mountains and along the Apishapa River between Walsenberg and La Junta. Bighorns have also been restored to historic ranges along the Purgatoire River east of Trinidad and along Carrizzo Creek south of Kim.

Some of the most productive bighorn herds in Colorado range in the mountains that encircle the San Luis Valley. Large herds occupy the Sangre de Cristos (north of Medano Pass), Trickle Mountain (north of Saguache), and the La Garitas north of Creede. Small bands are scattered throughout the San Juan Mountains, east of the continental divide, from Del Norte to the New Mexico line.

Bighorn herds that support limited hunting are found west and south of Aspen to Crested Butte and Gunnison. Bighorns range along the Taylor River east of Gunnison and are visible during winter along Highway 306 from Almont upstream about 8 km (5 miles). Finally, small herds of sheep are scattered throughout the San Juan Mountains near Lake City and Silverton, along the headwaters of the Piedra and San Juan Rivers, and south of Wolf Creek Pass to New Mexico.

Rocky Mountain National Park. Sheep generally range in the Never Summer Mountains and the Mummy Range in Rocky Mountain. Bighorns may be found throughout these ranges, but the most reliable locations are listed below.

Summer:	Winter:
Mount Richthofen	Sheep Lakes
Thunder Pass	Above Highway 34
The Crater on Specimen	from Fall River
Mountain	Entrance to Devils
Milner Pass	Gulch Road
Sites along Trail Ridge	Bighorn Mountain
Road	Above Endo Valley
Iceberg Pass	Acces Road
Rock Cut	
Sundance Mountain	
Lawn Lake Trail Head	
Sheep Lakes	
Lawn Lake	
Crystal Lake	
Hagues Peak	
Stormy Peaks	

Florissant Fossil Beds National Monument. Bighorns are most frequently spotted at Florissant during winter. The sheep seem to range throughout the southern portion of the monument, particularly west of the intersection of the lower Twin Rock Road and Teller County Road 1 and near the Sawmill and Hans Loop Trails.

Great Sand Dunes National Monument. While bighorns are found throughout the Sangre de Cristos, this monument does not provide much high-quality bighorn habitat. Bighorns can be observed on the south-facing slopes above the Medano Primitive Road approximately 1 km (1.6 miles) east of the monument boundary.

Bighorn sheep also are found in Dinosaur, Colorado, and Black Canyon National Monuments and Mesa Verde National Park. However, these bands of sheep inhabit remote, precipitous terrain and are only occasionally seen by visitors. It requires special effort to view bighorns in these federal parks.

Pronghorn Antelope
(Antilocapra americana)

Pronghorn antelope are a unique mammal, for they arose and evolved solely in North America. At one time in the distant past, antilocaprids had greater diversity than today, with as many as 10 or 12 genera (moose, elk, deer, caribou, etc., are all different genera of the cervid family). However, by the end of the Pleistocene glaciation, all but one genera had disappeared. Currently, there is only one representative of this family. Pronghorn are commonly referred to as antelope, but they are not even closely related to the true antelope of Africa. The translation of their scientific name is American goat-antelope, which again indicates their uniqueness.

Pronghorn were the delicate grazing partner of the bison on the prairies of North America. These slender animals stand 90 cm (35 inches) at the shoulder. Males weigh between 41-64 kg (90-140 pounds), females usually weigh about 25 percent less. Both sexes have horns covered by a black sheath; however, the horns of females are usually shorter than the ears. Horns of the males average 30 cm (12 inches) long and have a short, frontal protrusion called a prong, which arises from the upper half of the horn. The bucks shed their horn sheaths annually after the rut, usually in late November. Males also have a black cheek patch behind the lower jaw; females do not possess cheek patches.

Pronghorn are perhaps the most colorful North American ungulate. They are reddish tan on the upper parts of their bodies. The top of the snout and neck mane are black. The lower face is white, as are the sides, belly, and rump. Two bands under the neck are also white. The lower parts of the legs are blonde. The white rump patch is very large and the hairs erect if the pronghorn becomes alarmed. The entire rump patch serves as a very visible signal, alerting other members of the herd to danger.

Sign

Pronghorn tracks generally resemble those of mule deer, but are not heart shaped. The backs of the hooves are rounded and the tips narrow and squared at the ends. Remember, pronghorn have no dew claws; therefore, prints that show dew claws do not belong to pronghorn. Pronghorn tracks are about 5 cm (2.25 inches) wide and 7 cm (2.5 inches) long.

Pronghorn fecal material is pelleted and about 1 cm (0.4 inches) long. Pronghorn scat is not easily distinguished from deer pellets The presence of pellets in relatively flat terrain, far from trees and canyons, would generally alert one to the possible existence of pronghorn.

Occasionally, hikers may find shed pronghorn horn sheaths. Since pronghorn shed their sheaths in late November, the presence of horn sheaths indicates breeding areas and early winter range.

Breeding

Pronghorn breed during the month of September, and often the rut lasts only two or three weeks. Unfortunately, pronghorn are usually hunted during the rut, and this disrupts breeding. Pronghorn are very adaptable with their breeding system and, depending on resource availability, use either a territorial or harem-type system. In ranges where food and water resources are plentiful, bucks begin to defend a defined territory from other males by late summer. The strategy probably is to defend a territory which has sufficient resources to attract herds of does. Once they enter his territory, a buck will breed any receptive females and keep other males from entering. Once winter arrives, the buck will abandon his territory and join other pronghorn on the winter ranges. Where food and water resources are more dispersed, pronghorn bucks will defend harems of females rather than real estate. As the does move throughout the fall range, bucks will attempt to keep them herded together and fight other males trying to steal or breed females.

Twin fawns are usually born about 250 days after breeding. Fawns weigh about 3 kg (6.5 pounds) at birth and generally resemble adults in coloration. Even newborn fawns can be sexed at some distance, for buck fawns are born with black cheek patches. Pronghorn fawns are remarkably adept at lying still and hiding in the sparse cover of the grasslands. They are born with little scent and are inactive except when nursing. Their inactivity reduces the chance of being spotted by predators. At one week of age, the fawns are capable of outrunning a man and are weaned by late summer. Pronghorn mature quickly, some females actually breed as fawns. Males usually do not breed until they are two or three.

Habits and Habitats

Historically, pronghorn inhabited the prairies, sagebrush steppes, and intermontane grasslands of the west. Pronghorn ranged from eastern Kansas and Nebraska to California and Oregon and from south central Canada to central Mexico, including Baja, California. No one knows how many pronghorn ranged these areas, but they may have been as numerous as the bison, perhaps 30 million animals. However, market hunting and habitat destruction sent pronghorn numbers plummeting, and by 1920 only 13,000 pronghorn survived in the United States. After careful habitat management and legal protection was instituted, pronghorn numbers rebounded dramatically. Currently, about one-half million pronghorn inhabit the United States and Canada.

Today, pronghorn inhabit large grasslands and sagebrush steppes. While they may be found near timber, the timber is usually sparse and is used sparingly. Pronghorn have several adaptations which make them well suited to life in large tracts of wide open country. They have very large eyes and, correspondingly, very keen vision. Any moving object up to 1.6 km (1 mile) away cannot go unnoticed. Once danger is spotted, pronghorn cannot effectively hide themselves, for no adequate cover exists, nor are they large enough to defend themselves from enemies. Instead, pronghorn have developed incredible running abilities. No natural enemies of pronghorn can match their speed, let alone overtake them. When seriously threatened, pronghorn can attain speeds of 70-85 km per hour (45-55 miles per hour). Their cardiovascular system is designed to maximize air intake and oxygen delivery. Consequently, they can maintain high speeds for extended periods.

Why would pronghorn evolve the ability to run at such speeds when the fastest predator (wolves) can only attain 50 km per hour (30 miles per hour) over short distances? To understand the reasons behind this adaptation for speed, we must examine the predators that lived alongside Pleistocene pronghorn. Large dire-wolves roamed the same habitat as prehistoric pronghorn and no doubt were faster than modern wolves, due to their larger size. However, the predators that undoubtedly exerted the strongest selective pressures on pronghorn were cheetahs. A prehistoric cheetah evolved on the prehistoric grasslands alongside pronghorn and, by preying on the slower pronghorn, assured selection of the swiftest. Perhaps this is one reason why only one type of pronghorn survived. Although the prehistoric cheetah disappeared from North America, the swift pronghorn endured.

Pronghorn are also remarkably well adapted to foraging in the open grasslands and sagebrush steppes. They feed primarily on highly nutritious forbs and shrubs, yet little grass. Their digestive system is designed to take advantage of small, concentrated packets of food. The lips of pronghorn are split, and this permits them to be very selective in feeding on plants and even parts of plants. Remember, pronghorn had to share their habitat with bison; therefore, it was important that they minimized competition with bison. While bison feed on virtually anything in their path, pronghorn feed on only the choicest and less available foods. Pronghorn are also able to rely on sagebrush for winter forage. The oils that give sagebrush its characteristic aroma are poisonous to the rumen microbes. Although nutritious, most ungulates can only consume a small proportion of sagebrush in their diet because of its toxicity. Pronghorn, however, apparently consume as much as 90 percent of their winter diet as sagebrush. They, somehow, are able to handle the toxins and exploit a food resource largely unavailable to other ungulates.

Unlike other ungulates, adult female and male pronghorn herd together during the winter. Depending on winter severity, these herds can reach 500 to 1,000 individuals. These large gatherings are probably an anti-predator strategy. The larger the herd, the more eyes are available to watch for trouble and the smaller the probability any one individual may be taken.

Pronghorn have many enemies when young. Bobcats, coyotes, and golden eagles all kill fawns. In some areas, coyote and bobcat predation can be a limiting factor for pronghorn. Sometimes, does will attack coyotes in the vicinity of their newborn fawns. Golden eagle predation must be considered incidental; however, recent observations in Wyoming have verified that golden eagles are capable of taking adult pronghorn.

Pronghorn face two serious man-made threats today: fences and habitat conversion. Part of the reason pronghorn numbers rebounded after 1920 was the abandonment of farming homesteads throughout the west. These abandoned farms soon reverted back to grasslands and restored pronghorn habitat. Today, not only is urbanization usurping pronghorn habitat, but many grasslands throughout the west were converted to wheat croplands in the late 1970s and early 1980s. From Montana to New Mexico, acre upon acre of grassland was plowed under and converted to cropland. In Colorado alone, over 700,000 acres of prairie have been converted to cropland.

Livestock fences, if properly designed, do not hamper pronghorn movement. However, woven wire fences are barriers to pronghorn and can be devastating in winter. Pronghorn are forced to winter ranges by severe weather. If a fence blocks their path, hundreds will simply congregate at that spot and die from exposure and starvation.

Pronghorn can be legally hunted throughout the west. A lottery-type drawing is held for hopeful hunters and a limited number of licenses issued. Special archery seasons have been established for pronghorn, providing an exceptional challenge for bow hunters.

Locations

The most productive pronghorn herds in the central Rockies occur in Wyoming. Nearly 200,000 animals inhabit Wyoming and are readily seen from most highways that cross the state. Significantly fewer pronghorn inhabit Colorado. Current estimates indicate that 30,000-35,000 pronghorn live in Colorado. Pronghorn can easily be viewed at a distance from a vehicle; however, close observation is extremely difficult.

Although their distribution is not continuous, pronghorn range over the eastern Colorado prairies. Pronghorn can be viewed on the Pawnee and Comanche National Grasslands. Other good areas are Elbert, eastern El Paso, Lincoln, Kiowa, Pueblo, Huerfano, and Las Animas Counties. Pronghorn herds inhabit all intermontane parks in Colorado and are especially visible in North Park, north of Walden, during winter. Only a small relict herd currently lives in Middle Park. Pronghorn occur throughout South Park and the San Luis Valley. In the San Luis Valley, highest densities are found in Saguache county.

Perhaps the most productive herd lives in the northwest corner of Colorado. These animals range over all of Moffat county. Pronghorn habitat in Moffat county is very similar to Wyoming habitat and, therefore, these herds approach Wyoming's density. Not only are these herds larger, but many trophy males have been harvested from Moffat County.

Small pronghorn herds also exist north of Grand Junction, north and west of Delta, and south of Naturita. These desert-like habitats are not capable of supporting large numbers of pronghorn.

Rocky Mountain National Park. No pronghorn habitat is found in Rocky Mountain, although large herds once inhabited nearby Middle Park and a relict herd still maintains itself there. Pronghorn are visible in North Park, just outside the northwest boundary of Rocky Mountain.

Florissant Fossil Beds National Monument. Pronghorn are seen in the grasslands in and around Florissant. Pronghorn are most often seen in the northern and western portions of the Monument. Particularly good areas are north of the Cave Trail, south of the Upper Twin Rock Road, south of the Sawmill Trail, and near Hornbeck Homestead.

Great Sand Dunes National Monument. The National Park Service transplanted pronghorn into the Great Sand Dunes in the early 1960s. This herd is thriving and is visible in the brush lands south of the main dune field, west of the entrance road. Pronghorn are most visible between the dunes and the Mosca-Sand Dunes Road. Late summer and early fall are the best times to observe this herd.

Pronghorn do not live within the borders of Black Canyon or Colorado National Monuments or Mesa Verde National Park. However, they do inhabit and are visible in Dinosaur National Monument.

*Mule Deer in Velvet.
These bucks are hiding in
the cover of the krumholtz
zone. Note the red summer
coat and antler velvet.
Milner Pass, Rocky
Mountain National Park.*

*Mule Deer Buck. This
buck has descended to
the sagebrush type to find
breeding does. His antlers
are polished and gray
winter coat complete.
Beaver Meadows, Rocky
Mountain National Park.*

A. Adult Bull Elk. This breeding bull had exhausted his patience with me and was ready to charge. Fall River, Rocky Mountain National Park.

B. Young Elk in Velvet. This young bull is not large enough to successfully collect a harem. Note the antlers in velvet and red summer coat. Rock Cut, Rocky Mountain National Park.

C. Bull Moose. After stripping the velvet from his antlers, this bull continues to feed on willows in anticipation of the rut. Jackson county.

D. Bull Bison. This dominant bull takes time out from the rut to rest. Larimer county.

A.

B.

62

C.

D.

A. *Mountain Goat Billies. These subadult males scrambled down the cliff to investigate me. Note the white pelts and black horns. Mt. Evans.*

B. *Nanny and Kid. This family was ranging on the very top of the mountain when I found them. Mt. Evans.*

C. *Bighorn Rams. These rams tolerate each other's presence, for the moment. Specimen Mountain, Rocky Mountain National Park.*

D. *Bighorns on Winter Range. This group contains a mature ram, subadult rams, and mature ewes. Larimer county.*

B.

C.

D.

Pronghorn Buck. This old buck did not survive the following winter. Note his slender build and black cheek patch. Weld county.

Pronghorn Doe. This doe is healthy and ready for winter. Note the short horns and absence of cheek patch. Weld county.

SUGGESTED READINGS

Plants and plant communities:

Nelson, Ruth A. *Plants of Rocky Mountain National Park*. Estes Park, Colorado: Rocky Mountain Nature Association, 1976.

Harrington, *H. D. Manual of the Plants of Colorado.* Denver: Sage Books, 1954.

Willard, Beatrice E., and Ann H Zwinger. *Land Above the Trees.* New York: Harper and Row, 1972.

Tracking:

Murie, Olas J. *A Field Guide to Animal Tracks.* Boston: Houghton Mifflin Company, 1954.

Early Rocky Mountain National Park:

Mills, Enos A. *Wildlife on the Rockies.* Boston: Houghton Mifflin Company, 1909.

_____. *The Spell of the Rockies.* Boston: Houghton Mifflin Company, 1911.

_____. *The Grizzly.* Sausalito: Comstock Editions, Inc., 1919 (republished in 1981).

General Big Game:

Gilbert, Douglas L., and John L. Schmidt, Ed. *Big Game of America.* Harrisburg, Pennsylvania: Stackpole Books, 1978.

Coyote:

Jackson, H. H. T., and Stanley P. Young. *The Clever Coyote.* Harrisburg, Pennsylvania: Stackpole Books, 1951.

Wolves:

Mech, David L. *The Wolf: Ecology and Behavior of an Endangered Species.* New York: Natural History Press, 1970.

Young, Stanley P. *The Wolves of North America.* New York: Dover Publications, Inc., 1944.

Bears:

Craighead, Frank C. Jr. *Track of the Grizzly.* San Francisco: Sierra Club Books, 1979.

Herrero, Stephen. *Bear Attacks—Their Causes and Avoidance.* Piscataway, New Jersey: Winchester Press, 1985.

Bobcat:

Young, Stanley P. *The Bobcat of North America.* Lincoln, Nebraska: University of Nebraska Press, 1958.

Mountain Lion:

Young, Stanley P. *The Puma, Mysterious American Cat.* Washington, D.C.: American Wildlife Institute, 1946.

Mule Deer:

Wallmo, Olof C., Editor. *Mule Deer and Black-Tailed Deer of North America.* Lincoln, Nebraska: University of Nebraska Press, 1981.

Elk:

Thomas, Jack W., and Dale E. Toweill, Editors. *Elk of North America.* Harrisburg, Pennsylvania: Stackpole Books, 1982.

Bison:

McHugh, Tom. *The Time of the Buffalo.* Lincoln Nebraska: University of Nebraska Press, 1972.

Bighorn Sheep:

Geist, Valerius. *Mountain Sheep—A Study in Behavior and Evolution*. Chicago: University of Chicago Press, 1971.

Pronghorn:

Van Wormer, J. *The World of the Pronghorn*. Philadelphia: J. B. Lippincott, 1969.

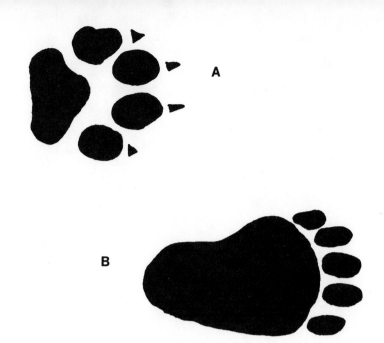

TRACK PATTERNS OF LARGE MAMMALS

A. Carnivore. This track is typical of canids. Cat tracks are round, show no claws, and the front of the heel pad is concave.

B. Bear. Hindprints of black bears leave no claw marks. The foreprint is similar, but the heel pad is square, not elongated.

C. Ungulate. Even-toed animals usually only leave tracks from two hooves. The dew claws are outlined here, but infrequently register.

About the author:

Stephen C. Torbit was born and raised on the prairies of southeastern Colorado. The son of a long-time Colorado family, Steve became concerned with conservation issues at an early age. He attended Colorado State University and earned degrees in chemistry, zoology, and a Ph.D. in wildlife ecology. Until recently, he was a full-time member of the research faculty in the Department of Fishery and Wildlife Biology at CSU. He owns his own wildlife photography business and has conducted wildlife ecology classes for local and national conservation groups. Steve retains an affiliate appointment at CSU, although he currently resides in Monte Vista with his wife, daughter, and two airedales.